C000065913

DIVINE GOVERNMENT

R T FRANCE

Divine Government

GOD'S KINGSHIP IN THE
GOSPEL OF MARK

First published in Great Britain 1990
SPCK
Holy Trinity Church
Marylebone Road
London NW1 4DU

Copyright © R. T. France 1990

All rights reserved. No part of this book may be reproduced or
transmitted in any form or by any means, electronic or
mechanical, including photocopying, recording, or by any
information storage and retrieval system, without permission in
writing from the publisher.

The translations from the New Testament are the
author's own; Old Testament quotations
are from the Revised Standard Version of the Bible,
copyrighted 1946, 1952, © 1971, 1973, and are reprinted by
permission of the National Council of the Churches of
Christ in the USA

British Library Cataloguing in Publication Data

France, R. T. (Richard Thomas), *1938–*
Divine government.
1. Bible. N. T. Mark — Critical studies
I. Title
226.306

ISBN 0-281-04471-6

Typeset by Pioneer Associates, Perthshire
Printed in Great Britain by
Dotesios Printers Ltd, Trowbridge, Wiltshire

Contents

———

Preface

The following pages represent the Moore College Lectures delivered at Moore Theological College, Sydney, in August 1989. They are printed more or less as they were delivered to an audience containing not only fellow academics and theological students, but also a good number who, while professing no specialist expertise in biblical studies, were eager to use the fruits of biblical scholarship to enrich their own theological understanding. In the hope that the lectures may be of interest to a similar range of readers in their published form, I have resisted the temptation to encumber them with more technical discussion and extensive footnotes. While the apparatus of technical scholarship has its due place, the value of such specialist discussion is surely questionable if its results cannot also be presented to a wider public in an intelligible non-technical form, as a positive contribution to Christian faith and living. I even dare to hope that it may sometimes be a pleasure to read!

I wish to record my thanks to the Principal and Staff and the whole Moore College community for their hospitality, and for a warmth of welcome which more than compensated for the loss of a few weeks of English summer. They were even (moderately) sympathetic to an Englishman's embarrassment at the state of the national game in the weeks when Australia regained the Ashes.

Dick France
Oxford, 1989

Introduction

The Kingdom of God – A Suitable Case for Treatment

One of the very few subjects on which there is near unanimity among New Testament scholars is the importance of the Greek phrase *he basileia tou theou* (conventionally but misleadingly translated into English as 'the kingdom of God'[1]) for an understanding of the teaching of Jesus, as it is recorded for us in the Synoptic Gospels. Few would doubt that this term, or its Aramaic equivalent, was a striking and distinctive feature of the teaching of the historical Jesus. It (or its Matthean equivalent 'the kingdom of heaven') occurs some seventy-five times (not including obvious parallels) in the Synoptic Gospels, and always in sayings attributed to Jesus. Moreover, these uses constitute over three quarters of the occurrences of the phrase in the whole New Testament.

While scholars debate the background and meaning of the phrase, ordinary Christians (and indeed even non-Christians) deploy it with great assurance and enthusiasm, as a convenient catch-phrase to sum up what they take to be the main thrust of God's work in his world. It is even commonly abbreviated into 'the kingdom', which is assumed to be something to which all Christians look forward and for which they live and work.

But *what is it?* If you press for a definition of what 'the kingdom [of God]' means, you are likely to be offered a variety of different answers, by scholars no less than by lay Christians. Some will use 'kingdom' language to promote world evangelization, some to demand a distinctively radical Christian lifestyle, some to campaign for social justice, some to challenge secular power politics, some to commend the rediscovery of charismatic gifts in the Church. And for many ordinary Christians the phrase, particularly in its Matthean

1

form 'the kingdom of heaven', does not relate to any situation on earth, whether present or future, but rather to the world to come. So language about 'the kingdom' is something of a rubber nose, capable of being twisted in any direction to suit the interests of the one who uses it. And that means that it offers fruitful ground for confusion and misunderstanding when the same phrases are used by people whose background predisposes them to interpret them quite differently.

The primary object of this book is to enquire what Jesus of Nazareth had in mind when he launched this powerful slogan on the world. What did *he* mean when he spoke about 'the kingdom of God', and what sort of ideas would such language have been likely to evoke in those who first heard him? How far was he taking up a theme which was already current in the world of his day, and how far challenging people to new ways of thinking and of responding to God as king? And how far does modern usage of 'kingdom' language correspond to what Jesus intended?

It would be naive to suppose that an appeal to return to the original understanding of *he basileia tou theou* can resolve the confusion in the use of such language today. Language (particularly religious language) does not work as simply or as mechanically as that. Usage can and must change to meet new situations and new ways of thinking. But when a term has become as many-faceted as 'the kingdom of God' is now, it must be worthwhile to look back to where it began, and to see how the various different strands in modern usage have developed out of (or have been superimposed on?) the understanding of Jesus' mission which he encapsulated in this term. If in the process some aspects of modern usage are found to be inappropriate, or even perverse, it is as well that we should be aware of the fact, even if this book cannot expect to change the linguistic habits of a generation!

The Gospel of Mark – A Suitable Starting-Point

It is clear from what I have said above that the place to begin a study of what Jesus meant by 'the kingdom of God' must be the Synoptic

Gospels. The phrase is virtually absent from the Gospel of John (only 3.3, 5 – though see 18.36–7 for the kingship of *Jesus*), while the few uses in the rest of the New Testament do not purport to record Jesus' usage, but that of his early followers.

Until shortly after the middle of this century most study of the Synoptic Gospels treated them largely as an undifferentiated whole, a total pool of 'synoptic tradition' from which scholars aimed, by means of appropriate critical procedures, to reconstruct aspects of the life and teaching of Jesus. With the rise in popularity of 'redaction criticism' in the 1960s all that changed, and Matthew, Mark and Luke came to be recognized as individual communicators, even theologians, each with his own contribution to make to our total understanding of Jesus. Further waves of critical fashion (structuralism, narrative criticism, etc.) have served to reinforce this approach, by concentrating attention not on the tradition underlying the Synoptic Gospels, but on the literary form and function of each of them considered as a finished work. It has therefore become less usual now to treat the three books as more or less equivalent witnesses to a single tradition.

It is interesting, however, that discussion of the very central theme of the kingdom of God still tends to be carried out largely on a 'pan-synoptic' basis. Books with titles such as *The Kingdom of God in the Teaching of Jesus*[2] have tended not to give separate attention to the three synoptic evangelists, and specific studies of the kingdom of God in Matthew, Mark or Luke individually have not been frequent.[3]

Perhaps in the end there is not sufficient difference between the evangelists' presentation of the theme to justify separate treatment. But this book arises out of the conviction that there is nevertheless something to be gained by listening specifically to one of the three on his own.

But in that case, why Mark? Among the Synoptic Gospels it is Matthew who uses 'kingdom' terminology most freely, with some fifty uses of 'the kingdom of heaven' or related phrases over against a mere fourteen uses of 'the kingdom of God' in Mark. So there would seem to be richer pickings to be found in a specific study of the kingdom of heaven in Matthew, and in fact at a number of points in this book, particularly in the final chapter, I shall indicate some of

the areas where Matthew does seem to have a distinctive perspective
to offer. But I have chosen to focus here on Mark simply because of
the general agreement that it is he who offers us the earliest (or, to
use the unflattering language of scholarship, the 'most primitive')
account of the teaching of Jesus.

I am not one of those who hold dogmatically to the majority view
of late nineteenth- and twentieth-century scholarship, that Mark's
Gospel was written and circulated sufficiently far in advance of
those of Matthew and Luke for their authors to be able to use it as a
literary source in virtually its present form. I do not subscribe to the
simple 'Who-copied-whom?' approach to the Synoptic Problem. I
suspect that the situation was a good deal more complex and less tidy
than that. I think we may better understand Mark, Matthew and
Luke as at least partially parallel developments of a widespread Jesus
tradition in different parts of the Roman Empire, though with a
great deal of cross-fertilization which at some points took the form
of the exact reproduction of written accounts of sayings and events.
So in speaking of Mark as the 'earliest' account, I do not necessarily
wish to suggest a linear progression whereby Matthew and Luke
'used' Mark.[4] But it does seem clear to me that Mark's is a more
limited, and in some ways less developed, record of Jesus, and for
that reason a suitable starting-point for an attempt to get as close as
we can to what Jesus himself taught, and thought, about the kingdom
of God.

And in fact, even though the phrase 'the kingdom of God' occurs
relatively infrequently in Mark, he himself encourages us to see it as
an important clue to the mission of Jesus, by the prominence that he
has given to it at the very outset of his narrative. We shall be
considering in Chapter One the significance of the opening
pronouncement by Jesus, 'The time has been fulfilled and the
kingdom of God has come near; repent and believe the good news'
(1.15). Mark's whole book is about the 'good news' of Jesus (1.1),
and that good news is here summed up in the announcement that
the kingdom of God has come. So this is not just a passing phrase, it
is the focus of the whole message of Jesus as Mark understands it,
and of the good news to which he invites his readers to respond.

I believe that our study of the ideas underlying this phrase as
Mark records it will show that this is a suitable way in to our

understanding of Mark's message as a whole, and that the infrequent occurrence of the phrase belies the central importance of the theme of God's kingship in Mark's theology. To understand this theme is therefore a promising route towards an appreciation of why Jesus chose to explain his central purpose in such language, and of what he meant by it.

Reading Mark as Mark

I mentioned above the tendency in recent discussion of the Gospels to treat them more seriously as individual works, each with its own distinctive message to convey in the way it presents the words and deeds of Jesus. This tendency represents a healthy reaction against the form criticism which dominated study of the Gospels in the earlier part of this century, which by focusing on the individual 'pericopes' (individual stories about Jesus or brief units of his teaching) easily fostered the impression that the Gospels were merely anthologies of Jesus traditions, with little more than a rudimentary scheme of arrangement to hold them together. On such a view it was easy to conclude that it did not much matter in which Gospel a particular unit of tradition occurred, nor how it related to other neighbouring units. Its meaning derived not from its present gospel context but from its original *Sitz im Leben*, which it was the business of the scholar to reconstruct as accurately as possible.

It must be admitted that this atomistic approach to the reading of the Gospels encouraged by academic form criticism has tended to be reinforced also by the Bible-reading habits of many Christian people. The Gospels are divided into suitable portions for daily devotional study (which frequently approximate closely to the 'pericopes' demarcated by form criticism), and thus a miracle or a parable or a section of instruction is read as a self-contained unit, without much regard to its context, and without considering that the evangelist may have placed it in that particular relation to his other material in order to throw light on how he expects it to be understood. Too often preachers have followed the same pattern of selecting gospel incidents or sayings to preach on in isolation, thus reinforcing the anthology model for the Gospels. The possibility that the evangelists wrote their books to be read as wholes (probably out loud in the congregation), and that they designed them in such a way that the hearer would be led effectively from theme to theme, building up the total picture in the manner of a good novelist, seldom occurs to us.

It was no doubt at least partly for this reason that when Alec McCowen started his solo recitations of the complete Gospel of Mark as a theatre performance the British public was captivated. Mark's 'anthology' could now be seen in a new light, as a well-told story, full of vivid description and humour, a work of mystery and tension, a dramatic whole building up to an inexorable and yet paradoxical climax. The result was a new appreciation of Mark as much more than a collector of traditions – but also a new understanding of the gospel story itself and of its central character, as a wholly believable and yet utterly astounding person engaged in a unique mission which even hardened Christians found themselves understanding in a new way.

But that was how Mark was meant to be appreciated from the beginning, and it is one of the most exciting aspects of recent gospel studies to see this original purpose coming increasingly into focus. 'Narrative criticism', with its focus on the unity of the text and the flow of the plot, is now firmly established.[5]

This book represents such an attempt to 'read Mark whole'. Not that the whole of Mark's Gospel is here under consideration. The study is limited to one theme, though a central one. In pursuing the theme of the kingdom of God we shall be focusing in some detail on several key passages in the Gospel, particularly those few places where the actual phrase 'the kingdom of God' occurs. But all the time I shall try to keep in view Mark's total project, and to interpret the individual passages as parts of the whole. Sometimes this attempt will lead us away from the direct terminology of the kingdom of God, as we explore the wider theological terrain within which this terminology belongs. Always I shall try to make sense of a passage not simply in terms of its own wording but also in its context within the flow of Mark's story. The result will, I hope, be not only a study of the fourteen uses of 'the kingdom of God', nor even a wider study of kingship ideas in the Gospel, but an encounter with the essential dynamics of Mark's understanding of Jesus and his mission, which he has chosen to encapsulate in 1.15 in the phrase 'the kingdom of God'.

In attempting to 'read Mark whole' I shall also try as far as possible to read him on his own terms. Christian readers who are familiar with the Gospels tend naturally to merge their separate accounts into one, and tend unconsciously to read Mark in the light of the way Matthew and Luke have presented their parallel accounts. Few think it important to notice in which Gospel a particular incident or phrase occurs, or to ask why there are differences in the way an apparently parallel tradition is recorded. But if we are to do justice to Mark's distinctive message, we must try to read Mark on Mark's terms. In this book I shall therefore make a deliberate attempt not to assume what Mark has not himself included, and not to read his words with a Matthean or Lucan accent.

At times, where it is important to be aware of the differences between the accounts, I shall refer to them and discuss why the evangelists tell their stories in different ways, but this will be with the aim of listening more intelligently to Mark's own distinctive voice. Not that I wish to portray the evangelists as engaged on incompatible enterprises, still less to turn differences of perspective gratuitously into contradictions. But it is only as we listen conscientiously to the different accounts individually that we shall be in a position to appreciate the whole impact of the total witness of the Gospels.

Mark's Gospel is a book of surprises, for its original readers most of all, but also for those who today are prepared to listen to it on its own terms, not cushioning its impact by the inherited assumptions of centuries of Christian familiarization. Mark's Jesus astounded and bewildered those who heard and saw him in Galilee, and he is still capable of challenging those who thought they had him comfortably pigeon-holed. I do not flatter myself that I have the skill or the insight of Mark, but I hope that this small tribute to his genius may help some to a new awareness of 'the secret of God's kingship' as it was revealed in 'the good news of Jesus the Messiah, the Son of God'.

1

God Rules!

Setting the Scene

Mark's story of Jesus begins with a brief paragraph or two in which he sets the scene for the narrative which will follow.[1] 'The beginning of the gospel of Jesus Christ the Son of God' is found in a composite quotation of Old Testament texts (Mal. 3.1; Exod. 23.20; Isa. 40.3) about the herald who prepares the way of the Lord, texts which awakened the Jewish expectation of the 'day of the Lord', the day when Israel's God would come in power to dispense salvation and judgement, the day of his indisputable rule over his world. In the larger-than-life figure of John the Baptist, the second Elijah, that herald has come, and the people of God have begun responding to his call to repentance in preparation for the great day of judgement. But John was only the herald; there was a 'stronger one' to follow, whose baptism would not be the merely outward washing of water, but the inward rebirth which is the mark of the coming of God's Holy Spirit.

'And in those days Jesus came . . .' The simple repetition of the verb 'come' in verses 7 and 9 says it all. The herald has done his work; now it is time for the real work of salvation and judgement to begin. Yet it is not, as Malachi and Isaiah had led people to expect, God himself who appears in irresistible splendour among his people, but 'Jesus from Nazareth in Galilee' (Where?!), and he comes as one among the penitent and expectant crowd to John's baptism. Here is the paradox which runs throughout Mark's Gospel, and which will be central to our study of it, the paradox of the hiddenness of the 'great and terrible day of the Lord', of power and authority effectively deployed where men would least expect it, visible only to the eye of faith.

And who is this unknown northerner among the Judaean crowds? He has the commonest of names,[2] and he appears on the scene like Melchizedek, without father or mother. His home is the humblest village of a provincial region little known or liked among the Jews of the Judaean heartland (cf. John 1.46, and that was spoken by a Galilean!). His human credentials are nil.

But 'immediately' (Mark's great word of emphasis) things begin to happen and a new dimension is introduced into the story. He sees heaven torn apart, and the Spirit of God descending upon him, while a voice from heaven declares him the Son of God. There are rich pickings to be found in a careful study of the words which the heavenly voice uses when seen against their Old Testament background,[3] but the legitimate delight of pursuing every nuance of allusion must not distract us from the main point: the unknown has been identified, and among the penitent crowd stands the one for whose coming they are so earnestly preparing. He knows it, and we know it (because Mark has told us), but they do not.

As Mark's narrative develops, we, with our privileged inside knowledge, shall be able to look on as the actors in the story grope their way towards this fundamental truth. Deep divisions will appear among the people of God, resulting from their various responses to Jesus. Many of them (especially the Judaeans) will miss the truth about Jesus altogether, and he will finish up in Jerusalem rejected and crucified by the very people he came to save. Many more will be slower to make up their minds, and even at the end of the story will still be unsure. But a few Galileans will begin to recognize the amazing truth of what is happening among them, and will become his followers, sometimes weak and hesitant, often misguided in their zeal, always struggling with God's paradoxical way of fulfilling his ancient promises, but gradually moving towards the great truth which Mark has already presented to us, his readers, in his prologue.

And 'immediately' the curtain is drawn aside a little further, and we see Jesus in the wilderness, the place of Israel's beginnings and the focus of her hope (see, e.g., Jer. 2.2–3; Ezek. 20.35ff.; Hos. 2.14–15). It was in the wilderness that John's revival movement had begun, and it must be in the wilderness that the day of the Lord will dawn (Isa. 40.3; 43.19ff., etc.).[4] But Jesus is not alone in the wilderness. Mark presents him in a tableau of symbolic characters:

on the one side Jesus led by the Spirit and sustained by angels, on the other Satan and the wild beasts.[5] The hostility of Satan to the work Jesus has come to accomplish is focused in the theme of 'testing', though the subject of that testing is not spelled out. The point the reader is expected to note is that Jesus' mission as Son of God is one which will be contested. Behind the human drama lies a cosmic conflict; the kingdom of Satan is under threat.

The Focus of Jesus' Mission

So far Mark has not begun his story; all this was introduction. Jesus has been little more than a passive figure on the stage, even though the centre of attention. The scene has been set, with the focus on the supernatural dimension which will underlie Jesus' mission. We, the readers, have been alerted to the issues at stake, and given the clues we shall need to understand the story as it unfolds. Now it is time to begin.

We begin with the removal of the herald from the stage, in the arrest of John. The introductory scene, located in the wilderness, is over, and Jesus appears in what will be the main theatre of his brief appeal to Israel, in Galilee. Galilee will be the focus of his activity right up to the final, fateful journey to the south, to Jerusalem, and it will be to Galilee that he will direct his disciples for the continuing of his mission after the resurrection (14.28; 16.7). So it is in Galilee that the good news must be proclaimed at the outset of his mission, and in 1.15 Mark presents in capsule form the burden of that mission:

'The time has been fulfilled and the kingdom of God has come near; Repent and believe the good news'.

This pronouncement could hardly be more clearly highlighted. Its literary position focuses all our attention on it as the beginning of the narrative for which the prologue has prepared us; its presentation as a brief key-note statement before the action proper indicates its programmatic function; and its language echoes just those scriptural expectations which the preceding verses have been fostering, the hope of the eschatological coming of God for which his people have long been waiting.

At the heart of this ringing declaration is the phrase 'the kingdom of God'. It is no wonder, then, that this phrase is generally regarded as summing up the message of Jesus. It looks as if Mark so intended it. But to agree that this phrase focuses Jesus' message is not necessarily to agree on what it means.

'Kingdom' Language

In modern Christian parlance 'kingdom' has become a 'buzz-word'. Its meaning is regarded by some as so self-evident that it has now come to be used as an adjective, as in the recent book titles *Kingdom Mercy*, *Kingdom Ministry*, *Kingdom Living.*[6] Recently I even saw a van bearing the legend 'Kingdom Car Service', to which no further elucidation was thought necessary other than the exhortation to 'Seek first the kingdom of God', painted over the cab door. I do not know what the unchurched passer-by would have made of it, but I was not sure whether the owner was offering to service my car in a distinctively 'kingdom' way (whatever that means), or to transport me to heaven!

Behind this odd adjectival use of 'kingdom' must lie the assumption that 'the kingdom' is a phrase with a clear meaning on which Christians can so far agree that the word itself evokes the intended context of meaning. But Christian understanding of the meaning of 'the kingdom of God' is not so uniform, even where any clear understanding is present. For some the phrase points to a desired socio-economic reform; for others to a distinctively charismatic style of discipleship; for others it points in an other-worldly direction, so that the phrase is virtually a synonym for heaven.

It is, then, questionable how far the adjectival use of 'kingdom' actually achieves any effective communication, except perhaps within a clearly defined circle where a particular 'in-group' usage has been agreed. But it is open to more serious objection than that, in that such usage purports to be based on the language of the New Testament; indeed the reason for the positive 'vibes' which 'kingdom' language is intended to produce is that anything so labelled is assumed to be distinctively biblical. It functions as a sort of hallmark whereby the genuine article can be distinguished. But 'kingdom' used adjectivally is not a biblical idiom, and I am not at all sure that the phrase 'the kingdom' is much better, even though hallowed by constant use in both scholarly and popular Christian writing. Let me explain.

The New Testament writers hardly ever refer to 'the kingdom', but rather to 'the kingdom of God' (except that Matthew uses the more Jewish form 'the kingdom of heaven'). The only New Testament uses of 'the kingdom' in absolute form to refer to what elsewhere is called 'the kingdom of God' are in Acts 20.25 (as the subject of Paul's preaching) and in three phrases where Matthew abbreviates his normal term 'the kingdom of heaven' when it depends on another noun ('the gospel of the kingdom', 4.23; 9.35; 24.14; 'the word of the kingdom', 13.19; 'the sons of the kingdom', 8.12; 13.38). Of these, Acts 20.25 is the only passage where it is fair to see an anticipation of the modern usage of 'the kingdom' as a phrase expected to convey a clear reference in itself. The New Testament phrase is clearly not 'the kingdom', but 'the kingdom of God'.

But surely it must be pedantic to insist that we use the exact biblical terminology. Where is the harm in a convenient abbreviation? I hope I am not usually a pedant, but in this case I do see a significant danger in the nearly universal modern use of 'the kingdom', a danger which is writ large when 'kingdom' comes to be used as an adjective. The danger arises from a twofold misunderstanding.

Firstly, the word 'kingdom' does not convey in modern English what the Hebrew/Aramaic *malkut(a)* and the Greek *basileia* conveyed in their biblical context. It is a scholarly commonplace to point out that whereas 'kingdom' in English is today primarily a 'concrete' noun, with a clearly identifiable 'thing' to which it refers (whether a place or a community), the biblical nouns are abstract, and refer to the *act* of ruling, the situation of being king – as did the word 'kingdom' in the sixteenth-century English from which it has entered our biblical tradition.[7] Hence the various attempts of scholars to substitute such terms as 'reign', 'rule', 'kingship', or 'sovereignty' for 'kingdom', attempts which are generally regarded as well-intentioned, but which have yet to affect general usage significantly, even within the scholarly fraternity.

The second point follows naturally. If 'the kingdom of God' means 'God being king', then to abbreviate it to 'the kingdom' is to focus on the wrong one of the two nouns. To speak of 'kingship' without saying *who* is king is to speak only in a vague abstraction which can have no specific reference in itself. 'The kingdom' is about as meaningless as 'the will' or 'the power' used alone without a reference to whose will or power is in view. To make the point in terms of a familiar biblical text, 'Yours is the kingdom, the power and the glory' (Matt. 6.13) does *not* mean that there are antecedent self-existent 'things' called 'the kingdom', 'the power' and 'the glory', which have come into God's possession. It means simply, '*You* are the king, *you* wield power, and *you* are glorious.' It is a statement about God, not about 'the kingdom'. The content of the phrase is no less than the great declaration of many Old Testament psalms, 'The Lord is king', or 'God rules'.

Thus the noun which determines the meaning of the phrase 'the kingdom of God' is not 'kingdom' but 'God'. It points to *God* in control, *God* working out his purpose. It is for this reason that B. D. Chilton paraphrases 'the kingdom of God' by 'God in strength', and points to the usage of 'the kingdom of God' in the targum (Aramaic paraphrase) of Isaiah to convey 'God's dynamic presence', 'the saving revelation of God Himself', 'God's actual exertion of royal force'.[8]

The point is right and important, but the phrase offered hardly works as a substitute for many New Testament uses of 'the kingdom of God'. (Can one 'enter' God in strength?) But the point can be made less dramatically by using a more clearly 'active' noun than 'kingdom'. One interesting use is that of G. R. Beasley-Murray, who, while using the phrase 'the kingdom (of God)' in relation to New Testament usage, heads each main part of his discussion with the phrase 'the coming of God';[9] but while this brings out clearly an important aspect of the Jewish context of Jesus' 'kingdom-of-God' language, it obscures the notion of control which 'kingship' involves. Subsequently Beasley-Murray offers the helpful paraphrase 'the saving sovereignty'.[10]

In the title of this book I have offered the phrase 'divine government', as another way of avoiding the unfortunately territorial or institutional implications of 'kingdom', while retaining its dynamic focus. But even if this phrase has the merit of making us rethink what we mean by 'kingdom', it is no more likely than others to be totally satisfactory as a substitute in each New Testament usage. However, I am not too concerned about exactly what word or phrase is used, so long as the focus remains in the right place. In what follows I shall speak often of the 'kingship' of God, and shall avoid 'kingdom' as much as I can, simply in order to reinforce the points just made. Above all, even though I think I know what Luke meant in Acts 20.25, I beg to be excused from submitting to the convention of speaking about 'the kingdom'!

'The Kingdom of God' in Mark

A brief overview of how 'kingdom of God' language is used in the Gospel of Mark may help to bring into focus what I have been saying about this terminology in the New Testament in general, and at the same time will prove useful as a background for the study which will follow.

The first, and obvious, point to be made in the light of the preceding discussion is that Mark never refers to 'the kingdom' in the way that Luke does in Acts 20.25. Wherever the reference is to God as king the full phrase *he basileia tou theou* is used.[11]

The verbs associated with the phrase reveal something of its dynamic connotations. It can be the subject of active verbs, as in 1.15, where it 'has drawn near', and 9.1, where it 'comes with power'. In the two parables of chapter 4 where the kingdom of God is explicitly mentioned as the subject of the parable, it is portrayed in terms of its active force, as the seed which grows (without human help!), in 4.26–9, and as the tiny mustard seed which produces a great shrub for the birds to nest in, in 4.30–2. Its independent coming and growth mean that people's response must be to wait eagerly for it (15.43) and to welcome it (10.15). But there is no suggestion that they can achieve it, or even hasten its coming. They may enter it (9.47; 10.23–5), or be close to it (12.34). The privileged disciples may know its secrets (4.11), and it belongs to little children (10.14). Then there is a rather different use in 14.25, where the phrase refers to the coming new situation in which Jesus will again drink wine.

In the preceding paragraph it has been grammatically necessary to refer to the 'kingdom of God' as 'it', but there is no obvious 'thing' to which the phrase refers. Rather it points to *God*, who has drawn near to save, who exercises his power as king, and whose dynamic activity is described in the parables of growth. It is God's saving work that people wait for and welcome. The 'kingdom' into which they enter, and which the privileged few understand and possess, is a relationship with God himself, so that, for instance, 'to such belongs the kingdom of God' in 10.14 could be paraphrased, 'God is their king'.[12] And the 'kingdom of God' in which Jesus will again drink wine points to a new situation still to come, when God will have achieved his purpose and his rule will be finally established.

These linguistic associations of the phrase indicate a breadth of use which defies neat systematization. The one thing which is common to them all is *God*. As God the king exercises his authority in his world, and people respond to it, there the 'kingdom of God' will be experienced in many ways. There can be no one place, time, event or community which *is* 'the kingdom of God', any more than 'the will of God' can be tied down to any specific situation or event. 'The kingdom of God' is God in saving action, God taking control in his world, or, to use our title, 'divine government'.

It will be the aim of the rest of this book to unpack some of the rich content which Mark has included in his use of this phrase, as a key to his understanding of what it was that Jesus came to do. In order to do that we must first return to Mark 1.15, and ask what effect such language might have been expected to have had when Jesus first proclaimed the coming of God's kingship in Roman Galilee.

God's Kingship and the Hope of Israel

I have devoted some space to discussing the way 'kingdom' language is used in modern Christian parlance, and the way in which this differs from the usage of the New Testament, because unless this difference is exposed it is possible for modern readers to come to such texts as Mark 1.15 with a preconception of what 'the kingdom of God' means which has little to do with what Jesus' hearers might have been expected to make of it. Now it is time to return to what Mark (and Jesus) *did* mean. And for that purpose we must consider the background against which such language would have been understood by Jews at that time.

Another scholarly commonplace is that 'the kingdom of God' is not a phrase which was in common use either in the Old Testament or in the literature of inter-testamental Judaism. As a statistical observation about the incidence of the actual phrases *malkut YHWH, malkut ha-shamayim*, etc., this is undoubtedly true, and Jesus' frequent use of the set phrase, to the extent that it becomes a virtual slogan of his ministry, was a striking innovation. But that does not mean that his hearers had no background against which to interpret such language. Indeed it was the argument of Norman Perrin's suggestive account of 'the kingdom of God' as a 'symbol' that such a phrase served to evoke all that was most fundamental to the national self-consciousness and hope of the Jews as the people of God.[13] Subsequent scholarship has reinforced that argument, in particular the exciting tracing by George Beasley-Murray of the theme of 'the coming of God' through the Old Testament and through the writings of early Judaism.[14] Once we break free of the extraordinary notion (sadly still common in biblical interpretation) that the development of a concept may be analysed simply by tracing the usage of a given phrase, it is possible to recognize the kingship of God as a fundamental belief and hope of the Jews.

To be the people of God was to recognize God as king. As creator, he was king of the whole world, and it is this universal kingship which the psalms so memorably celebrate: 'The Lord reigns; let the earth rejoice . . .' (Ps. 97.1); 'The Lord reigns; let the peoples tremble!' (Ps. 99.1); '. . . the Lord is a great God, and a great King above all gods' (Ps. 95.3). It was this fundamental assurance which formed the basis of Israel's theology. It was also a cause of pride and wonder that such a God had chosen Israel to be his people. King of the whole earth as he was, he was nonetheless in a special way the king of Israel. This theocratic ideal did not easily accept the rise of a human monarchy (1 Sam. 8), and the human king must continue to recognize that he owed his authority to his divine appointment. In theory at least, the priest and the prophet, as representative and spokesman of God, had authority over the king, so that the basic truth of God's kingship was not forgotten.

God's kingship, so understood, was a present fact, not merely a hope for the future: his reign is eternal. But no sensitive observer of the world has ever been able to believe that 'everything in the garden is lovely'. Theology may declare that God is king, but experience begs to differ. Israel's human leaders proved to be weak and corrupt, and foreign powers who owed no allegiance to the God of Israel increasingly took control of their destiny. Worship declined into empty formality, and righteousness was at a premium. The prophets, for all their faith in the eternal sovereignty of God, not only denounced the arrogance of men but puzzled over the apparent inactivity of God. Surely this was not what the kingship of God was meant to be like.

So the kingship of God became not only an accepted datum but also, paradoxically, a hope for the future. The day was still to come when every knee would bow before the one true God and his perfect world-order would be established, when Yahweh who was already king *de jure* would be seen to be king *de facto* (e.g. Isa. 45.23; Zech. 14.9). This hope of the effective establishment of God's kingship underlies the development of messianic expectation in the Old Testament, and especially the growth of apocalyptic thought and writing, in which it increasingly takes the form of an imminent and catastrophic intervention of God in the affairs of a world gone wrong.

The most striking development of such expectation in the Old Testament is in the book of Daniel, and it is here, appropriately, that the language of kingship comes most clearly to the fore. Indeed, 'the theme of the book of Daniel is the kingdom of God'.[15] The narratives are set in the courts of the kings of Babylon and Persia, the human rulers of the world, and they focus on the conflict between human authority and divine. The sovereignty of God is seen vindicated in one episode after another, and even the mighty Nebuchadnezzar is forced to acknowledge the Most High, the 'King of heaven', as the one whose 'kingdom endures from generation to generation', and from whose hand alone his own kingship is received (4.34–7). But within this setting Daniel's visions look forward to something more ultimate, to the replacement of all human empires by the one unshakable kingdom represented by the stone 'cut out by no human hand' which shatters the great image of human imperial power (2.31–5), and by the 'one like a son of man' who comes on the clouds of heaven to the throne of God and is given 'dominion and glory and kingdom' over all nations for ever (7.13–14). The spotlight is moved away from earthly events *per se* to the supernatural world of conflicting powers which lies behind them, a change of focus which makes a mere restoration of Davidic rule inadequate and incongruous, and calls for a new level of understanding of how the kingship of God is to be realized.[16]

Daniel's visions formed the inspiration for much later apocalyptic hope, and scholarship is increasingly recognizing their formative influence not only on Jesus' use of the title 'the Son of Man' but also on his language about the kingdom of God. Two recent studies from different perspectives have underlined Daniel's seminal influence (and in so doing have put down a strong challenge to the view prevalent in German scholarship that the concepts of the Son of Man and of the kingdom of God are unrelated and incompatible). George Beasley-Murray's study of Jesus' sayings about the kingdom of God devotes an introductory chapter to 'the coming of God in Daniel 7', and includes a full study of the Synoptic Gospels' Son of Man sayings as a necessary part of a study of the kingdom of God.[17] Chrys Caragounis' massive study of the Son of Man presents 'the Kingdom or Rule of God' as the central theme of Daniel, and concludes that 'the Son of Man and the Kingdom of God are in Jesus' teaching indissolubly connected with each other, as they were in Daniel'.[18] In our study of Mark we shall see how strongly the language and ideas of Daniel have influenced the teaching of Jesus about the kingdom of God.

In subsequent Jewish thought both main streams of Old Testament belief about God's kingship remained alive and important. God's eternal kingship is assumed in such texts as Wisdom 6.4 (human kings are 'servants of God's kingship') and 10.10 (Wisdom showed Jacob God's kingship and taught him knowledge of holy things). The great seventeenth Psalm of Solomon pleads for a restoration of Davidic kingship on the basis that 'Lord, you are our king for evermore . . . the kingdom of our God is for ever over the nations in judgement' (Ps. Sol. 17.1, 3, 34, 46).

But while no one would have disputed this theological truth, language about God's kingship increasingly points to the future (and preferably the near future!). The eschatological hymn of Testament of Moses 10 begins:

> Then his kingdom will appear throughout his whole creation.
> Then the devil will have an end.
> Yea, sorrow will be led away with him . . .

and goes on to describe the cosmic signs accompanying God's coming, which will result in the elevation of Israel over her enemies. Similarly the Qumran seer declares that in the coming battle when the Sons of Light are to be vindicated over the Sons of Darkness the dominion of Satan will be destroyed and 'the kingship will belong to the God of Israel, and he will exercise his power through the holy ones of his people' (1QM 6.6).[19]

Such hopes were not confined to special visionaries either. The regular synagogue liturgy at the time of Jesus already concluded with words which he himself would echo in the prayer he taught his own followers to use:

> Exalted and hallowed be his great name in the world which he created according to his will. May he let his kingdom rule in your lifetime and in your days and in the lifetime of the whole house of Israel, speedily and soon.[20]

This was the prayer of every pious Jew, of men such as Joseph of Arimathea, who, as Mark tells us, 'was looking for the kingdom of God' (15.43).

So when Jesus came into Galilee declaring that the time had arrived and God's rule was about to begin, he was not speaking in a vacuum. While people no doubt varied in their understanding of how God's kingly authority was to be exercised, they were already praying for that time to come.

But this was not, as far as our texts enable us to judge, a hope for the betterment of the world in general; it was a prayer for the restoration of *Israel*, as the chosen people of the one true God, to the place of pre-eminence among the nations which had barely survived the reign of the first great king, David. After centuries of subjection to pagan powers, Jews looked not just for God to be glorified but, like Simeon, for Israel to be vindicated (Luke 2.25). Recent New

Testament scholarship has been increasingly alive to this dimension
of the context into which Jesus came with his message of the
kingship of God.[21] Ben Meyer's important study of *The Aims of
Jesus* points strongly in this direction:

> . . . dissociation of 'the reign of God' and its proclamation from 'the
> restoration of Israel' is *a priori* implausible.
>
> Scholarship ought never to have lost sight of this basic correlation.
> In the biblical perspective salvation was always and everywhere
> understood as destined precisely for Israel. 'Salvation' and 'Israel'
> were utterly inseparable. There was never a Saviour apart from a
> saved Israel, nor would there be a Messiah apart from messianic
> Israel . . . Israel, in short, understood salvation in ecclesial terms.[22]

In this context a declaration of the coming of the kingship of God
was inevitably understood in nationalistic terms. It puts the message
of Jesus into the same frame of reference as the appeal of the various
factions of Jewish freedom-fighters whom we conveniently lump
together under the later party name 'Zealots'. How far Jesus' message
coincided with that of the Zealots will be our concern later, but
there can be no doubt that it was in relation to their ideology that his
proclamation was bound to be assessed.

The Zealots were, in the words of Gerd Theissen, 'radically
theocratic'.[23] As we have seen, all Jews were theocratic in theory;
but for Judas of Galilee that theory must be translated into political
action when a pagan power claimed dominion over the people of
God. He 'incited his fellow-countrymen to rebellion, and called
them cowards for putting up with Roman taxation and thus tolerating
human domination when God had been their true king'.[24] So the
Zealot movement was born out of the theology of the kingship of
God. The revolutionary violence against the Sons of Darkness
which for the Qumran seer was merely an idealistic vision had
become a practical policy of military action. God's kingship must not
only be hoped for and prayed for, but also fought for.

Such a 'radically theocratic' ideology commanded significant
popular support, and would lead a generation later to the disastrous
war against Rome. But that war was to reveal deep divisions among
the Jews, and already at the time of Jesus' preaching we must not
assume that Judas' simple logic was universally accepted. It would
be simplistic to imagine that language about God's kingship would

have a single clear meaning for Jews then (any more than it has for Christians today). But 'the kingdom of God' was not a newly coined term waiting to be filled with whatever meaning Jesus chose. It already carried deeply significant connotations, and was well calculated to set his audience buzzing with enthusiastic expectation, however varied those expectations may have been.

To take this already loaded language and to mould it to his own particular understanding of his mission was a risk Jesus had to take. 'Putting it simply, Jesus had to use terms which were understood by his contemporaries or they could not have understood him at all; but he had to use them differently, if he was to say something new.'[25] That dilemma, the inevitable lot of anyone who wishes to change people's thinking and understanding, will underlie much of our study in the rest of this book of the use of the language of divine kingship in the Gospel of Mark.

Mark 1.15 – 'God is Taking Over'

We have seen that Mark begins his book with a prologue designed to appeal to Jewish expectations of the fulfilment of the hopes of Israel, and to point to Jesus of Nazareth as the one in whom that fulfilment is to be focused. At the same time he has alerted his readers that the stage on which the drama is to be played is not merely that of human relationships, even of national politics, but of the cosmic encounter of the Son of God with the kingdom of Satan.

The story then begins with a ringing public declaration of the purpose of Jesus' mission, and at the centre of that declaration is the key phrase 'the kingdom of God'. In this phrase all the idealistic hopes of the people of God find expression, and Mark's readers, if they are Jews, no less than Jesus' hearers in Galilee, can hardly avoid the conclusion that the time of Israel's restoration has arrived. Yet already in the prologue the note of paradox has been struck, and Mark's story will continue to surprise, and to challenge his readers, whether Jew or Gentile, to rethink their understanding of how God is to exercise his kingship. The establishment of divine government through the ministry of Jesus of Nazareth is not going to fit the expectations of the actors in the story; supporters no less than opponents will find themselves bewildered by him. And we the readers, even though the prologue has given us a privileged glance behind the scenes, must none the less prepare to embark on a voyage of discovery in which many of our presuppositions will be challenged and our attitudes changed to accommodate the revolutionary values of the kingdom of God.

One of the more interesting proposals for a modern 'dynamic equivalent' for 'the kingdom of God' in Jesus' teaching comes from David Wenham.[26] He suggests that Mark 1.15 might be paraphrased, 'The revolution is here!' What the Old Testament pointed forward to was 'God's revolution', and it was that revolution which Jesus was announcing and implementing. I believe this proposal has more merit than may appear at first sight. The word 'revolution' seems calculated to shock, and makes the apolitical Christian hearer uneasy. But is that not exactly what Jesus' 'kingship of God' language was bound to do? 'Kingship', no less than 'revolution', is a political term; and to establish a kingship which is not as yet effective *is* to bring about a revolution. Of course revolutions vary, and it is to be expected that a divine revolution will not be marred by the worst aspects of human political action which make the word 'revolution' so suspect to us. But it is none the less revolutionary for that. Indeed, as we shall see in Chapter Three, the revolutionary demands of Jesus' preaching of God's kingship are far more searching than mere political radicalism. Jesus *was* preaching revolution, and the phrase in which Mark has summed up his message means no less.

But it is, as David Wenham is at pains to explain, *God's* revolution, and Mark's use of 'kingdom of God' language makes this very clear. There is, as we have noted, no reference in Mark to 'the kingdom' as if it were a 'thing' in itself. It is 'God' that is the controlling noun. The message of Mark 1.15 is not that a change of government is imminent, but that *God* is taking over (which potentially puts a question mark against any human political programme, even a Jewish one). Thus Ben Meyer, noting that the Aramaic targums use the phrase 'the reign of God' as 'a reverential circumlocution for "God" (as ruler)',[27] continues: '"the reign of God" was both intended and understood to have immediate reference to God's own saving act . . . "The reign of God" signifies "God" and signifies God precisely as Jesus knows him.'[28] Indeed Joachim Jeremias goes so far as to say, 'When Jesus announces *engiken he basileia tou theou*, his meaning is virtually "God is near". This is what people will have heard in the call of Jesus: "God is coming, he is standing at the door, indeed, he is already there".'[29]

Now or Not Yet?

But *is* he 'already there'? To be the herald of the imminent arrival of God in his revolutionary, saving power is not the same as to proclaim him as already present. Or, to put it in the more traditional terms of New Testament debate, does Mark 1.15 present God's kingship as future (though imminent) or as already realized? In this classic discussion attention has rightly focused on the verb *engiken*, which may be literally translated 'has come near'. It is in the perfect tense, which suggests something more decisive than merely 'is coming near', or 'is at hand'. In their commentary on Matthew, W. F. Albright and C. S. Mann attempted to 'capture the urgency' of the verb by the translation 'is fast approaching', but it is interesting that Mann, in his subsequent solo commentary on Mark, finds it necessary to change to 'is upon you' in order to convey the 'note of immediacy'.[30] The same tense of the same verb is used in Mark 14.42 to announce the presence of Judas, whose arrival is narrated in the next verse.

Translations of *engiken* have varied in relation to the individual scholar's commitment either to 'futurist' or to 'realized' eschatology in the teaching of Jesus, but what has not always been sufficiently noted is that the phrase does not stand alone, but is preceded by 'The time has been fulfilled', another perfect tense, this time of the verb *pleroo*. *Engizo* means 'to come near', not in itself 'to arrive', so that even in the perfect tense it may be felt to retain some sense of expectation; but *pleroo* points precisely to the realization of what was expected or promised, and its perfect tense here can be interpreted of a future event only if the *kairos* referred to is the time *of waiting* rather than the time of God's action – and that would be an odd use of *kairos*, which is traditionally distinguished from *chronos* precisely as the decisive moment rather than mere passage of time. On any normal understanding of the Greek, then, the clause which *precedes* 'the kingdom of God has drawn near' has already stated explicitly that the decisive moment has arrived.

For what it is worth, then, my vote at the end of this particular exegetical debate would be for those who see Mark 1.15 as a declaration of arrival, not just of imminence.[31] But I wonder whether the debate was not rather misdirected in the first place.

It has, of course, long been recognized that the debate in New Testament scholarship between 'futurist' and 'realized' eschatologies can never be solved by a 'victory' for either side, since both elements are clearly present in the New Testament. Hence the more recent formulae such as 'inaugurated eschatology', 'eschatology in the process of realization', or 'consummation without fulfilment'. These represent a clear step in the right direction, and convey an important truth for the understanding of the New Testament, that its authors seem to have no difficulty in holding together the 'already' and the 'not yet' in their presentation of God's saving work. But in so far as the debate has focused specifically on the kingship of God, it has too often proceeded on the basis of the misconception we considered above, that 'the kingdom' must refer to a particular situation, event or time. It then becomes necessary to locate that situation or event within a chronological scheme of *Heilsgeschichte*. But when it is recognized that the New Testament is not talking about a 'thing' called 'the kingdom', but about God reigning, the whole question loses its focus. 'The kingship of God' is not the sort of phrase about which it is easy to ask, 'When is it?' To be sure, against its Jewish background the phrase encapsulated a clear hope of future change, and to announce that it has come is to lead people to expect things to be decisively different. But this is not to require that there must be a precise moment before which it is not and after which it is a new reality. God, who is eternally king, will work out his purpose in history, and so his kingship will be seen to be exercised progressively as his rule is more widely accepted and honoured. But he is no less king in the earlier stages than in the later.

So I am not too worried whether Mark 1.15 is interpreted as locating God's kingship just before or just after the moment of announcement. It both 'has come' and 'is coming', just as in the longer version of the Lord's Prayer we can balance 'Your kingdom come' with 'Yours is the kingdom'.[32] The main point of Mark 1.15 is not the precise timescale, but the fact that it is *in the coming of Jesus* that we are to see God's revolution taking place. Indeed, it is *in Jesus* that we are to see God coming as king.

In the following chapters we shall be exploring how Mark leads his readers to grasp this truth, and to work out its implications for their own response to 'the coming of God'.

2

Government Secrets

Mark 1.16—3.35 – A Surprising Sequel

Mark's story of Jesus has begun with a prologue (1.1-13) which alerts his readers to the Old Testament hope of the coming of God to save his people, which introduces Jesus of Nazareth in the wilderness, the place of hope and of new beginnings, which associates him closely with the Spirit of God, and which has already identified him as no less than the Son of God. When such a prologue has been followed by a striking declaration by Jesus that the decisive time has now arrived, and God's kingship has come near, no reader who is at all sensitive to Jewish hopes in first-century Palestine can fail to be prepared for a dramatic sequel. It is something of a surprise, therefore, that the phrase 'the kingdom of God', introduced with such prominence in 1.15, does not occur again until chapter 4, and then in a way which hardly seems to match the expectations aroused by the opening of the book.

What we do see in chapters 1—3 is Jesus collecting a small group of men of no social prominence, and entering with them on an itinerant ministry among the villages and small towns of Galilee.[1] Within this limited arena Jesus' activity is undoubtedly impressive. His success as a healer and exorcist is repeatedly noted, and people remark on his unique 'authority' (1.22, 27; 2.10-12). His reputation spreads around the whole area (1.28, 45), and large crowds gather wherever Jesus goes, to hear him preach and to see and benefit from his power over physical and spiritual evil (1.32-4, 37; 2.1-2, 13; 3.7-10, 20; 4.1). Some of the crowd even come from outside Galilee (3.7-8), and we are introduced (ominously, as later events will reveal) to a group of scribes who have come from Jerusalem, apparently specifically for the purpose of investigating Jesus' activities (3.22; cf. later 7.1, an equally hostile group of 'investigators'). So Jesus is making a mark, at least at the local level, and his reputation is spreading. But this is not yet the stuff of which revolutions are made, and those who were now keyed up to expect the immediate coming of God to save his people might have been forgiven for wondering whether the Jesus movement was really what they were looking for, however much they may have been caught up for a time in the excitement of the moment. The kingship of God has not yet very obviously arrived.

If we are to understand chapter 4 of Mark's Gospel, and the things that it says about God's kingship, we must keep this background in mind. There is some explaining to be done. The credibility of Jesus' initial announcement of the beginning of divine government is in question.

One prominent feature of these early chapters of Mark (and one which will recur throughout the Gospel) is the variety of ways in which people respond to Jesus and his ministry. In chapter 1 the mood is overwhelmingly positive; Jesus is popular and sought after, though there is a difference between the few fishermen who leave all and follow him (1.16–20) and the larger synagogue congregation which is intrigued and excited, but remains puzzled (1.21–8). But already before the end of chapter 1 there is perhaps a hint of opposition in Jesus' command to the cured leper to go to the priest and make the appropriate offering 'as a testimony to them' (1.44) – does this suggest that the religious establishment figures may need some convincing?

What may be hinted at in 1.44 becomes clear and prominent in the following episodes. Jesus is accused of blasphemy by the local scribes (2.6–7), and 'the scribes of the Pharisees' disapprove of the company he keeps (2.16). The contrast between Jesus' 'open house' approach and the more restrictive demands of traditional religious observance is giving rise to questions about his orthodoxy (2.18–22), and his attitude to sabbath observance is positively scandalous (2.23–3.6). Already by 3.6 the point has been reached where the religious and political interests of (respectively) Pharisees and Herodians coincide in the determination to get rid of Jesus. He is too uncomfortable – and too popular.

For the Pharisees and the Herodians do not yet represent the ordinary people. The crowds glorify God for what they see in Jesus, even in the face of the accusation of blasphemy (2.12), and the outcasts make him welcome (2.15–17). When Jesus withdraws from the scene of conflict (3.7) it is not alone, but with 'a great multitude' of supporters. No doubt many of them were there, as Mark suggests, primarily to benefit from his healing power, but some at least are prepared to go further in their commitment to the new Jesus movement, and Jesus is able in 3.13–19 to select an inner circle of those who are prepared 'to be with him' and to share his preaching and delivering ministry.

And there is yet another response which Mark includes for the sake of his readers, who have been made aware in the prologue of the wider dimensions of Jesus' mission. Jesus' exorcisms are not just acts of mercy towards tormented people; they represent the onslaught on the powers of evil which is the necessary obverse to the establishing of the kingship of God. *People* may see only a preacher and healer, but the demons recognize Jesus for who he is, 'the Son of God' (3.11). This is knowledge which we the readers are allowed to share, but the actors in the story are not, because Jesus strictly charges the demons not to speak, 'because they knew him' (1.34; 3.12). Jesus has come, as the Son of God, to fulfil a public mission in bringing in God's kingship among his people, but the only characters in the drama who have yet really grasped the truth are forbidden to reveal it. It is this paradox which chapter 4 will aim to explain.

But before we get to chapter 4 Mark has another remarkable section in which all these strands are brought together, and the divisions which are being created by Jesus' ministry are brought even more clearly into focus. In contrast with the inner circle of committed disciples (and the contrast will be made explicit in 3.33–5) we see two groups who in differing degrees reject Jesus. The extreme of opposition is represented by the Jerusalem scribes, who attribute Jesus' work of deliverance to the power of Satan, and allege that he is himself demon-possessed (3.22, 30). Here is the ultimate perversion of the truth about Jesus, the blasphemy against the Spirit of God which can never be forgiven (3.28–9). But framing this episode, in 3.21 and 3.31–5, is the first introduction of Jesus' family.[2] Their view of Jesus is perhaps marginally less offensive, but no less dismissive – he is mad! The scene then finishes with the poignant vision of Jesus surrounded by the 'circle' (literally, v. 34) of his followers, with the members of his natural family standing 'outside' that circle (vv. 31, 32) – and this language of insiders and outsiders will be picked up in chapter 4. Here it is spelled out in the striking pronouncement that Jesus' true mother and brothers are not the natural family who reject his message, but 'whoever does the will of God' (v. 35).

In the course of this symbolic scene, the language of kingship has again been introduced. But this time it is not the kingship of God which is mentioned but, by implication, the kingship of Satan (it is explicit in the parallel in Matt. 12.26). In his response to the charge of the Jerusalem scribes, Jesus ridicules the idea of 'Satan against Satan', on the grounds that no 'government' (*basileia*) could survive on that basis (vv. 23–6). But if they have been wrong in lining Jesus up on the side of Satan, they are quite right to see his mission in the light of Satan's kingship. It is that kingship that he has come to destroy, but he will do it not by division within but by direct assault from without. The binding of the strong man so as to be able to plunder his possessions (3.27) is a parable of the essential focus of Jesus' mission. The exorcisms which have already been recorded as one of its central features (1.23–7, 32–4, 39; 3.11, 15, 22) are part of the victorious irruption of the kingship of God into the kingship of Satan.[3] The new age of God's government has begun. In far more than a political sense, the revolution is here!

But yet Jesus does not want the demons to give away the secret of his identity, and people can see his powerful ministry and draw from it very different conclusions.

And so into this atmosphere of secrecy and paradox, but yet of the powerful working of God's kingship for those with eyes to see, Mark introduces in chapter 4 one of his longest and most integrated collections of Jesus' teaching,[4] the parables of the kingdom of God.

In Parables

Chapter 4 contains three stories that would fit everybody's definition of a parable, those of the sower (vv. 3-8, 14-20), of the growing seed (vv. 26-9), and of the mustard seed (vv. 30-2). Of these the last two are explicitly attempts to explain what the kingdom of God is like, while the explanation of the parable of the sower is introduced by a comment on the revelation of 'the secret of the kingdom of God'. The subject of these three parables may therefore fairly be said to be the kingdom of God.

It is now agreed, however, that our modern tendency to use 'parable' only of more or less extended illustrative stories does not cover the whole range of the Greek *parabole*, so that the 'many things in parables' which Mark mentions in 4.2, 'the parables' which the disciples asked about in 4.10, the 'everything in parables' of 4.11, the challenge to understand 'all the parables' in 4.13, and the 'many such parables' offered to the crowd in 4.33-4 clearly include more than these three little stories (and the other three such 'parables' in our restricted sense which Mark includes elsewhere in his Gospel: 12.1-12; 13.28-9; 13.34-7).[5] Mark himself has already described Jesus' teaching about the kingdom of Satan in 3.23ff. as being 'in parables', and chapter 4 contains other epigrammatic sayings (which is a part of the meaning of *parabole*) which also serve to set the challenge of God's kingship before his hearers - the lamp under the tub and 'measure for measure' (4.21-5).

So 'in parables' does not mean merely 'in the form of illustrative stories', though of course it includes that meaning. Parables may better be understood more broadly as the opposite of prosaic, propositional teaching. Parables, in this broader sense, attract attention by their pictorial or paradoxical language, and at the same time their indirect approach serves to tease and provoke the hearer. It would be possible to hear a parable as no more than an interesting story or a striking *bon mot*, and entirely to miss the point. Parables offer images and riddles which we must work out for ourselves if we are to understand and respond. Parabolic teaching is not given on a plate. It demands perception and careful thought, and it challenges to appropriate action.

C. F. D. Moule appropriately compares New Testament parables to the modern political cartoon.[6] The picture alone may please and amuse, but if that is all that happens the cartoon has failed. To appreciate it requires some knowledge of the current political scene, and the willingness and perceptiveness to work out the principles the cartoonist wished to illustrate, and to respond in appropriate action. The more you bring to it, the more you get out of it. So it is also with parables (as indeed Mark 4.24–5 states quite clearly).

Such an indirect method is eminently appropriate for teaching about God's kingship. There is, as we have seen, an element of paradox and of surprise built into this subject. God's method of government does not correspond to human expectations, and it takes such striking and teasing language to jolt people out of their unexamined presuppositions, and to open them up to God's revolutionary values. 'The general tendency of parables . . . is to confound our conventional and comfortable world view: to shake us out of complacency and imperviousness to the challenge of the Kingdom or the Word. Their demand is therefore far-reaching and more likely to be evaded than welcomed.'[7]

Such demanding teaching carries with it, then, the probability that not all will be equally able to appreciate and respond to it; some will be enlightened and changed, some will be offended and will react with hostility, while others are left unaffected beyond a vague and benevolent interest. The coming of God's kingship, and its revelation 'in parables', is thus going to leave people divided.

That division is a central theme of chapter 4. Chapters 1–3 have revealed a growing polarization in people's response to Jesus and his proclamation of God's kingship, and chapter 4 goes on to clarify and to explain this division by setting out the 'secret of the kingdom of God'. The three story-parables portray that 'secret', and one of them (the sower) explains in some detail why people are so divided in their response; the notorious teaching about the purpose of parables in 4.11–12 (together with the further comments on Jesus' teaching method in 4.33–4) draws out the implications of this division for the further development of Jesus' ministry; and the epigrams of 4.21–5 challenge the hearers to respond appropriately to the revelation of God's kingship.

Three Images of God's Kingship

The three story-parables of Mark 4 are all concerned with the growth of seed. They thus portray the kingship of God as something dynamic rather than static, something which will be strikingly different at the end from what it was perceived to be at the beginning. The parable of the mustard seed (4.30–2) especially focuses on the element of surprise, of paradox, in the final size and importance of the mustard plant in contrast with its insignificant beginning, 'smaller than all the seeds on earth'. Of course any seed would have illustrated the fact of quantitative growth, but the choice of the mustard reveals where the focus was intended to be, since mustard seed was proverbially *tiny* (cf. Matt. 17.20; Luke 17.6; Mishnah, *Niddah* 5.2).[8] The parable thus speaks to those who could not take seriously an announcement of God's kingship which was so apparently insignificant, the message of a small group of countrymen in a backward province. By normal human standards it *is* ludicrous to make such a claim, but that is what God's kingship is like. It turns human valuations upside down, and thrives on paradox. That is why its coming is inevitably a 'secret', unknown and unrecognizable to those who cannot view it in the divine perspective.

The dynamic power of God's kingship is the obvious point also of the parable of the growing seed (4.26–9). The emphasis falls on the ability of the seed to grow *by itself*. The farmer can go away and live his own life while the seed gets on with its growth; he doesn't know, and doesn't need to know, how it does it. The earth looks after the process *by itself* (*automate*), and all the farmer will need to do is to reap the crop which has been produced for him without his own effort. Any real-life farmer will tell you, of course, that it is not as simple as that, that life between sowing and reaping is not simply an extended holiday. But a parable is not necessarily a photographic reproduction of real life, and the story is clearly told in such a way as to emphasize the lack of human involvement. God's kingship has its own dynamic, and is not dependent on human effort. It is, in other words, *God's* saving power which is the subject of Jesus' message, not a human reform programme.

Both these parables of growing seeds, then, warn Jesus' hearers of the danger of interpreting God's kingship by human standards, and therefore of failing to appreciate the significance of what is happening through his ministry. There is a secret here to be discovered. God is powerfully at work, but many will be unable to see it. But those who despise and even oppose Jesus' mission are in for surprises. And those who want to believe him but are tempted like John the Baptist to ask 'Are you really the one we were waiting for, or should we look for someone else?' (Matt. 11.3) may take heart: God's work *will* be completed, in *God's* way. In both parables there is an impressive harvest to come, however unpromising or incomprehensible they may find the period of growth.

The parable of the sower also ends with a bumper harvest. Scholars argue about whether 'thirtyfold, sixtyfold and a hundredfold' is merely an extraordinarily good natural harvest, or whether it represents the miraculous fruitfulness of an earth transformed by the eschatological coming of God.[9] But in either case there is a sense of the effective working of God; as in the other parables, his kingship produces results. In this story, however, the foil against which the triumph of God's purpose is set is neither the smallness of the seed nor the inactivity of the farmer, but the unpromising variety in the soil. In spite of the various setbacks resulting from the state of the soil, the farmer may none the less look forward to a rich harvest. So when the gospel of God's kingship is preached in the world, people will vary in their response to it. Some will barely listen at all, some will respond with initial enthusiasm which has no staying power, and some will lose interest as other concerns compete for their attention. It would be easy for the observer to write off a movement of such varied fortunes, and for its converts and missionaries to lose heart in the face of such setbacks. But this parable, like the other two we have considered, assures them that God really is in control, and that there will be a great harvest.

But is that all there is to it? The varied nature of the soil is so carefully analysed and so structurally prominent in the way the story is told (and no less so in the point-by-point explanation which follows in each of the Synoptic Gospels) that it is not improper to suggest that this variety is really the main focus of the parable. It is often assumed that the whole emphasis is on the harvest, and that, in the light of A. Jülicher's famous insistence that a parable must have only one point, all the detail of the different soils must be regarded as inessential scenery.[10] But while Jülicher's protest against the allegorical interpretation of parables was much needed at the time he wrote, it is generally agreed today that his dogmatic insistence on one point per parable was an over-reaction. Where a parable is deliberately constructed as a series of episodes, each of which is carefully depicted in its own right, there is nothing fanciful (or 'allegorical') in suggesting that each is to be noted and pondered as part of the total message of the parable. Thus Moule argues that the sower should be understood as a 'multiple parable'.[11] And if that is so, the synoptic interpretation of the parable, which has so often been written off as a subsequent moralizing *mis*interpretation, can better be seen as picking up at least one aspect of the intended purpose of the parable, perhaps even its main point.[12]

If we are, then, intended to take note of the different characteristics of the four types of soil which form the framework of the 'story', the position of the parable in Mark's Gospel becomes important. We have seen how the first three chapters have set out the variety of ways in which people have responded to Jesus and to his preaching of God's kingship, and how the carefully balanced scene which concludes chapter 3 has raised with particular force the question of who in this situation are and are not the true people of God. Faced by a large crowd (4.1–2), and no doubt one which included people with varying degrees of enthusiasm and commitment towards his message, Jesus now analyses the range of response, and warns of the danger of half-hearted commitment. It is not only the total rejection of the message (as by the Jerusalem scribes in 3.22ff.) which will result in fruitlessness, but also the failure to allow the message of God's kingship to penetrate deeply and to take first place in his followers' allegiance. The same demand for whole-hearted response will recur in the epigrammatic sayings of 4.21–5, and there, as at the end of the parable of the sower, the challenge will be launched, 'He who has ears to hear, let him hear.'

So woven into the parable of the sower is the theme of division, which has been at the forefront of the narrative in the preceding two chapters. The division results from, or at least is reflected in, the differing ability of people to hear and respond to the message. Not all, apparently, *have* 'ears to hear'. It is this theme of divided response which is picked up and examined in the saying about 'the secret of God's kingship' which follows the parable in 4.10–12, and which leads into its explanation, words which have been more discussed (and disliked) than almost any other part of the Gospels.

Knowing the Secret

The parable of the sower, together with 'many things in parables', was spoken in the open air, to a 'very large crowd' by the lake (4.1–2). By the end of the parable section in chapter 4 a similarly large audience is still in view, as those to whom Jesus spoke with 'many such parables' are contrasted with the disciples to whom alone private explanations are given (4.33–4). But within this framework is a section beginning at 4.10 which is sharply contrasted as private teaching to the disciples, when Jesus is now 'alone' (*kata monas*, which presumably focuses more on the absence of the crowd than on total isolation). Mark does not indicate where this private teaching ends, as no change of scene is marked between 4.10 and the conclusion in 4.33–4. But since the point of verses 33–4 is that parables are given to the general public but explanation only to disciples, the private teaching must include the explanation of the parable of the sower (vv. 13–20), but presumably not the two other parables of verses 26–32, and probably not verses 21–5, which also contain parables rather than explanation, and include in verse 23 the same open challenge to respond with which the public parable of the sower concluded.

So in 4.10–12 Jesus helps his disciples to understand parables in general, and in verses 13–20 the parable of the sower in particular, while in verses 33–4 Mark adds his own comment on Jesus' teaching method. The inclusion of one detailed explanation of a parable could be viewed as merely a single illustrative example chosen at random, but the wording of verse 13 suggests that the parable of the sower was more than just one parable among many: if they cannot understand *this* parable then they will not understand any. That is why the parable of the sower comes first. It is the key parable, the parable about parables. The varying response to the sowing of 'the word' represents the way parabolic teaching works, leaving people divided. Indeed 'the word' which is sown *is* in the first place Jesus' teaching in parables, for that is the only sort of teaching which Jesus is offering to the wider public, as Mark points out in verses 33–4. So the explanation of the parable of the sower is tightly bound up with verses 10–12, and the whole section of private teaching in verses 10–20 is devoted to answering the disciples' question about 'the parables' (v. 10).

The theme of division runs through this section, not only in the contrasting of the different soils, but in the narrative setting which excludes the crowd from the disclosures of verses 10ff., and above all in the sharp distinction drawn in v. 11 between 'you', to whom the secret has been entrusted, and 'those outside', for whom there is nothing but unexplained parable to which, according to verse 12, they will be unable to respond. The language of 'insiders' and 'outsiders' picks up the preceding scene in 3.31–5, where Jesus' mother and brothers are twice described as 'outside' (3.31, 32), while those within Jesus' 'circle' (3.34) are twice described as *peri auton* ('around him'), the same phrase which is oddly used of the privileged group to whom Jesus' private teaching is given in 4.10, 'those *peri auton* with the twelve'. We shall return later to the question of just who constitute the two groups, but the outsider/ insider schema is clearly important for Mark's purpose.[13]

The difference between the two groups is one of revelation. The one group is given the secret, the other is not. I have used the term 'secret' because it conveys the meaning of the Greek *mysterion* more effectively than does the more traditional rendering 'mystery'. 'Mystery' in English suggests something which is in itself enigmatic, puzzling, hard to fathom; but the Greek *mysterion* focuses not so much on the nature of what is to be known, but on who knows it. The 'mystery' religions of the ancient world took their name from their esoteric character: their beliefs and practices were not necessarily very intellectually demanding, but they were secret, known only to initiates, whose duty it was to guard that knowledge from outsiders. While there is no reason to imagine that Mark's use of the word *mysterion* derives from a conscious echo of this pagan usage,[14] the sense of secrecy is essential to the meaning of the word. The message of God's kingship is not a 'mystery' in the sense that it is incomprehensible, but it is a 'secret' in that not everyone yet knows it. And to know the secret is something which is 'given' to some and not to others. It is not a matter of superior intellectual ability, but of divine revelation. Indeed the thrust of Mark 4.11 might better be conveyed by speaking of 'revelation', with its positive connotation of a privilege given, than of 'secrecy', which rather suggests a privilege withheld. But 'secret' is what *mysterion* means, so long as it is understood of a secret *shared*, not a secret guarded. It is a secret not because it is meant to be kept hidden (as 4.21–2 makes clear), but because no one can know it unless the knowledge is 'given' by God himself.

But that knowledge is not given to everyone, and Mark 4.11–12 appears to indicate that the inability of 'those outside' to understand is a matter of divine policy, which it is the purpose of Jesus' parabolic teaching to sustain. Parables, far from being means of enlightenment, are intended to hide the truth and keep the outsiders out. Can Mark, and Jesus, really be saying that?

Seeing Without Perceiving

The secret, we must remember, is the secret of *God's kingship*. And the parables of chapter 4 emphasize, as we have seen, that divine government does not operate on human lines. So long as what God is doing is assessed by human standards, it cannot be appreciated or understood; it will remain a 'mystery' (in the modern English sense), and the seed of the message will fall in unfruitful soil.

This is no new experience, for when God called Isaiah to his prophetic ministry he warned him that his preaching would be counterproductive, and Jesus' words in Mark 4.12 echo Isaiah's paradoxical calling. Indeed the wording of Isaiah 6.9–10 seems to suggest that absolutely no one will 'get the message' (though perhaps the 'holy seed' of Isa. 6.13 carries a promise of future response, and in fact Isaiah *did* gather disciples around him, Isa. 8.16). Mark 4.12 is an abbreviated version of Isaiah 6.9–10. But it omits the most shocking element in those verses, the command to Isaiah actually to 'Make the heart of this people fat, and their ears heavy, and shut

their eyes' (Isa. 6.10) so as to prevent their understanding and being
saved.

At least that is what the Hebrew text says. The LXX (quoted by
Matthew in his longer reference to Isa. 6.9–10 in this connection,
Matt. 13.14–15) softens the harshness of this language by turning
the command to the prophet into a statement about the condition in
which the people already are: their heart *is* fat, their ears heavy, etc.,
and that is why they will not be able to understand and respond. Is
the LXX, then, here squeamishly avoiding the offensiveness of Isaiah's
language by perverting a clear imperative into an indicative? Or is
such a suggestion merely a mark of what C. F. D. Moule calls 'a
pitiful literalism'? He goes on:

> It is difficult to believe that, in its original context in Is 6, it was
> intended as an instruction to the prophet to make sure that his
> message was unintelligible. Of course these are final clauses, as far as
> the grammar and syntax of the Hebrew go. But who seriously believes
> that such literalism was intended? It is only reasonable to take the
> final clauses as, at most, a vigorous way of stating the inevitable, as
> though by a very forceful indicative clause.[15]

If Moule is right, the LXX, while it may have lost some of the shock-
value of the Hebrew wording, has correctly interpreted its thrust.
And in that case the abbreviated Marcan version puts the emphasis
where Isaiah intended.[16]

But even so, the statement is terrible. People are, says God to
Isaiah, so conditioned that they will be unable to appreciate Isaiah's
message, and will be none the better for it. They can hear and see
indeed, but it goes no further. And when Jesus speaks to the crowds
the situation is no better. They hear the words and see the pictures
which the parables put before them, but it has not been 'given' to
them to penetrate their meaning.

It is remarkable that it is in connection with *parables* that this
statement is made. Surely parables are the one form of teaching of
which this ought not to be true. People might well fail to respond to
prosaic discourses and learned treatises, but are not parables fresh,
vivid, uncomplicated sayings, used to bring to life teaching which
might otherwise prove too abstract for ordinary people to grasp? Is it
not precisely the object of parables to break through people's

incomprehension, to produce that flash of insight which will turn
hearing into understanding?

But we must remember that 'parables' in biblical language are not
just simple visual aids. The semantic range of the word includes also
riddles and dark sayings, which puzzle and tease, and which do not
yield their secrets without special insight (see especially the use of
parabole in Mark 7.17). To say that for those outside 'everything
happens in parables' (literally, 4.11) is not to say simply that Jesus
offers them a series of helpful illustrative stories. It means that they
are confronted with enigma. Not necessarily with that which is
deliberately *made* obscure (as a literal reading of Isa. 6.10 might
suggest), but by a whole new situation which does not fit human
expectations, and which demands a mental and spiritual revolution
if it is to be understood. The phrase 'everything happens in parables'
(rather than 'is spoken in parables') suggests that it is not only Jesus'
teaching that is in view but his whole ministry. In what he does as
well as in what he says people are confronted with enigma. (Is it for
this reason that Mark has reversed the order of the clauses in Isa.
6.9, putting seeing before hearing?) The whole Jesus movement is,
in this sense, 'parabolic'. Its significance is not to be grasped by the
casual onlooker or dilettante. Its understanding is a matter of
revelation, a 'secret' which not all have yet come to share.

So there will be insiders and outsiders, as long as there are some
who have not responded to the good news of the kingship of God in
the ministry of Jesus. It is not Jesus' parables in themselves which
cause this division, but rather his whole ministry with its
revolutionary challenge. But it is in people's response to the parables
that the division is most clearly demonstrated, as their basic
orientation is revealed by their ability or inability to see things from
God's perspective. The division is not caused by the parables; it is
already there. This perspective is surely built into the parable of the
sower, where the problem lies not in the seed, but in the fact that the
condition of some of the soil is already unsuitable. So it was for
Isaiah, and so it was for Jesus and may be expected to be for those
who continue to preach God's kingship in a world which does not
want to know.

Predestined to Remain 'Outside'?

If the insight which the kingship of God demands is 'given' to some and not to others, whose fault is it that they do not understand? Those who are not let into a secret can hardly be blamed for not knowing it.

This is not the place to attempt an answer to the age-old problem of selection in the dealings of God with his people. But I think our discussion of Mark so far allows some relevant comments to be made. First, our study does not support the simple view that Mark presents Jesus as choosing to teach in parables as a means of keeping people out of the kingdom of God. Parables *reveal* people's inability to respond; they do not cause it. The problem lies further back than that. Nor is it simply the teaching method *per se* which has this result, but rather the whole character of Jesus' message and ministry as a challenge to abandon natural human insights and to see everything in the new perspective of God's kingship. Such a change takes divinely given insight, 'to know the secret of God's kingship'.

The aim of Jesus' preaching throughout Mark's Gospel so far has been to attract people to God's kingship, not to repel them. And he has had remarkable success. The 'insiders' to whom he is speaking in 4.10ff. were not always insiders. They had no more natural ability to penetrate the secret than 'those outside'. But through Jesus' ministry it has been 'given' to them. So if to them, why not to others? And indeed Mark offers us indications at other points in the Gospel that the division between insiders and outsiders is not a gulf which cannot be crossed (e.g. the scribe who is 'not far from the kingdom of God' in 12.34) and that the category of 'insider' may be more inclusive than some of his followers thought (e.g. the exorcist who 'was not following us', in 9.38–9, leading to Jesus' pronouncement that 'Whoever is not against us is for us', 9.40–1). If 'outsiders' can never become 'insiders', then the whole mission of preaching the good news of God's kingship is a cruel hoax. It can and does produce results, as the parables of chapter 4 make clear. The seed is sown and produces a crop beyond all expectation. But *how* the result is achieved is beyond human understanding, as we see in the parable of the growing seed (4.26–9). It is the work of God, not the result of the successful application of an approved technique, not even the use of parables.

But does the structure of chapter 4 offer at least the hint of another answer to the problem of selection? C. F. D. Moule believes it does.[17] He notices the unusual description of the 'privileged' audience of verse 10; they are not 'the twelve', or even 'the disciples' (though cf. 'his own disciples' in v. 34), but 'those who were about him with the twelve'. This, says Moule, 'is not a closed group but a chance gathering'. They are characterized as a group who ask questions, and it is this that differentiates them from 'those outside'. It was precisely such questions which the parables were designed to evoke, and they have succeeded. Some of the seed has fallen on good soil. While some were not interested to pursue Jesus' teaching beyond an initial hearing, others (who naturally included, but were not confined to, the twelve) wanted to know more. So they came and asked Jesus, and in so doing constituted themselves 'insiders'; to them, because they wanted to know, the secret was given. The division is the result, then, not so much of divine predestination as of self-selection.

I find this argument attractive, as far as it goes. I think it is based on a true perception of how parabolic teaching functioned in Jesus' ministry (and indeed still does), even though I suspect that Moule lays too much emphasis on the fluidity of the groups represented, in view of the clear divisions already emerging in chapter 3, the use of *peri auton* in 3.32, 34 to distinguish Jesus' circle from his puzzled family, and the specification in 4.34 that it was only to 'his own disciples' that Jesus explained his parables.

But even if Moule's argument is correct, this merely moves the same basic problem one stage further back, and we must still ask what it is that makes some ready to seek for new enlightenment when others are not. I do not think that chapter 4 of Mark's Gospel answers this question, nor do I think it was intended to do so. It shows how people respond to the message of the kingship of God, and clarifies the divisions which are already there in people's responsiveness to divine revelation. Some have 'ears to hear' and some have not. But chapter 4 does not attempt to explain *how* some soil comes to be good and some bad, beyond the general principle of the parable of the growing seed that God's work is achieved in God's way, not by human planning or effort. That God does turn some outsiders into insiders is the message of the whole New Testament, but this chapter does not allow us to investigate the process of selection.

If this seems an unsatisfying conclusion, it is, I hope, at least an exegetically honest one. Mark chapter 4 presents the selective revelation of the secret of God's kingship as a fact, but solutions to the problem of divine selection must be sought elsewhere. In so far as Mark 4 offers us any perspective on this problem, it lies in its insistence that an understanding of God's way of governing his world is never likely to be achieved by unaided human observation and logic. Experience confirms that such understanding is 'given' rather than achieved by argument.

Divine Government and Secrecy

Mark began his story with Jesus' open declaration of the inauguration of divine government and a public call to respond to this good news with repentance and faith. His narrative has shown people responding, typically in the four fishermen who left everything to follow him; and Jesus has been pursued by eager crowds who want to hear more of his teaching. After such a beginning, 'secret' is not the word we might expect to find associated with the next mention of God's kingship. Indeed, one of the 'parables' of chapter 4 insists that the light must be allowed to shine, and that secrets are there to be revealed (4.21–2).

Yet alongside this open declaration of God's kingship we have already begun to hear another theme, which will become increasingly powerful as Mark's Gospel progresses. Jesus was first introduced to us by the Jordan as the unrecognized 'stronger one', the messianic king and Son of God who comes from an obscure village as one of the penitent crowd. When his true identity is in danger of being revealed, he silences the demons who recognize him (1.24–5, 34; 3.11–12), and will not allow the healed leper to talk about his cure (1.44). When opposition arises, Jesus and his followers 'withdraw' from the place of conflict (3.6–7) and subsequently take to the hills for a time (3.13). Despite the parable of the lamp, there does seem to be an element of 'hiddenness' about Jesus' activity and teaching.

Since William Wrede first introduced it to gospel scholarship,[18] the phrase 'messianic secret' has come into common use for this aspect of Mark's portrait of Jesus. While Wrede's theory of a deliberate rewriting of history by Mark has been heavily and rightly criticized,[19] the data on which he based his theory must be important for any understanding of this paradoxical Gospel. And chapter 4 helps us to begin to understand the rationale of what has hitherto been a strange anomaly in the developing story.

At one level, a policy of secrecy was a political necessity. Jesus' message had already provoked murderous hostility (3.6), and where people are looking for ammunition to use against you, it is as well to choose your words carefully, and to control the unthinking enthusiasm of your supporters. It may be, then, that an element of simple prudence underlay not only Jesus' avoidance of publicity but also his decision to use the indirect teaching method of parables rather than straight declarations which could be turned against him.[20]

However, it was not only Jesus' enemies who were a problem, but also his friends. As the story develops it becomes increasingly obvious that much of the popular enthusiasm for Jesus and his preaching of God's kingship reflected not so much an understanding of his message, but precisely a *mis*understanding. We shall be returning to this theme later, but in view of what we have seen of the nationalistic sentiments which were likely to be evoked by 'kingdom of God' language in first-century Palestine, Jesus' 'secrecy' may well have been intended to avoid fostering the wrong sort of hopes about his leadership. A divine government which was not to be achieved by human effort and was to turn upside down human expectations was likely to have little to do with what 'the kingdom of God' would suggest to most of Jesus' contemporaries. Perhaps it is not so surprising then that the term has been conspicuously absent from Jesus' teaching in Mark since 1.15.

But yet 'Nothing is hidden except to be revealed, nor is anything concealed except to be brought to light' (4.22). The secret of God's kingship is already known to some, to whom it has been 'given' (4.11), and it is the object of Jesus' mission to add to their number. Once the seed has taken root, the understanding of divine government can grow, for 'He who has, to him will more be given' (4.25). Those who have responded to Jesus' preaching so far, and have become part of the circle of 'those about him', will gradually find their whole outlook and lifestyle revolutionized. It will be a long and painful process, and often their misunderstanding will be more prominent than their insight. But from these unpromising beginnings the mustard seed will grow until it becomes greater than all the other plants, and the birds can find shelter under its branches.

3

Revolutionary Government

'The Revolution is Here!'

In Chapter One I mentioned David Wenham's proposal that a suitable modern dynamic equivalent for 'the kingdom of God' would be 'the revolution', and his consequent paraphrase of Jesus' declaration in Mark 1.15 as 'The revolution is here!'[1]

Such a paraphrase would cause no surprise to many of those Jews who listened eagerly to Jesus' announcement. When the people of God were the unwilling subjects of a pagan power, held in check by the most powerful and efficient imperial system the world had yet known, it must have seemed self-evident that the effective re-establishment of divine government could take place only through a revolution. And many of them were keen to co-operate in that revolution, indeed to initiate it if a suitable occasion and leader could be found. The theocratic ideology and the economic grievances which swept the whole of the province into a disastrous revolt against Rome a generation later were already simmering in the Galilee of Herod Antipas no less than under the direct Roman government of Judaea and Samaria.

So Jesus' language of divine government could not fail to find an enthusiastic response. Revolution was in the air. But one man's revolution is not necessarily the same as another's, and the possibility of misunderstanding and of false hope runs throughout the story of Jesus' ministry, right up to its apparently inglorious conclusion on a Roman cross, the mark of a revolution which failed. This issue will remain in our sights throughout the remainder of this book, particularly in the last chapter, when we compare Jesus' role as Messiah with that of other revolutionary leaders. Indeed it has already been before us as we have traced the growth of division in

45

people's response to Jesus, and have begun to focus on the note of paradox which runs through Mark's presentation of Jesus' preaching of God's kingship. The true nature of that kingship is a 'secret', accessible only to those who are privileged to receive divine revelation; for others it remains 'in parables', an enigma.

As Mark's story continues it becomes increasingly clear that what makes Jesus' preaching of God's kingship so strange and so unwelcome from a natural human perspective is not that it is not revolutionary enough, but rather that it is too revolutionary. A 'revolution' which looks only for a change of human government by human means has not even begun to deal with the more deep-seated issues which are the concern of divine government. Putting it simply, human ideas of revolution themselves need to be revolution-ized.[2] It is this challenge which has already begun to be issued in the parables of chapter 4, and which will continue to sound throughout the Gospel. God's kingship will involve the overthrow of many aspects of the status quo, but it is remarkable that among those powers and values which it will challenge Jesus seems to have little interest in that aspect of the current situation which for many of his hearers was primary, the fact of Roman imperial government.

The Overthrow of Satan

The most fundamental level at which a divine revolution must take place is that of spiritual power. We have seen how Mark's prologue takes his readers behind the scenes, and enables us to glimpse something of the spiritual dynamics which lie behind the human drama, not only in the baptism scene, with its vision of heaven torn apart, the Spirit coming down and the voice of God declaring Jesus' true identity, but also in the confrontation of Jesus with Satan in the wilderness. No indication is given in the prologue of the outcome of that confrontation:[3] it merely stands as a reminder of the fundamental dimension underlying Jesus' mission. But the narrative soon shows Jesus in victorious conflict with spiritual powers (1.23-8), and this conflict remains a central feature of the story as it develops (1.32-4, 39; 3.11-12, 15, 22; 5.1-20; 6.7, 13; 7.24-30;

9.14–29, 38–40), so that an observer of Jesus' ministry as Mark records it must inevitably have seen exorcism as one of the major purposes of his mission.

The recurrent emphasis of the exorcism accounts is on the unique authority of Jesus. The demons recognize him as 'the holy one of God' (1.24), 'the Son of God' (3.11; 5.7), and are unable to resist his word of command. Whatever authority the demonic forces may have had is crumbling before the authority of the Son of God. Even if 1.12–13 did not present the decisive defeat of Satan, it soon becomes clear that his rule cannot survive the coming of Jesus.

So when the source of this irresistible authority is brought into question in chapter 3 by the scribes from Jerusalem, it is appropriate that the language of kingship is used. The 'parables' (3.23) with which Jesus refutes the charge that he is himself in league with Beelzebul begin with the common-sense observation that exorcism, as an attack on Satan's power, is hardly likely to owe its success to satanic inspiration! Even on the scribes' premise, Jesus' activity would be an act of rebellion against his supposed master, not of complicity. The argument is underlined by pointing out the disastrous effects of internal dissension on a 'kingdom'. Kings rule by the exercise of uncontested authority, and Satan is pictured as such a king. But the nature of Jesus' challenge to Satan's kingship is not that of a rebellious underling, but of a rival king intent on conquest. It is his purpose to tie up the 'strong man' and so to dispossess him (3.27). Thus in the ministry of Jesus God's kingship is being asserted over that of Satan.[4] A revolution is taking place, and a new government is being installed.

But the effect of this revolution in the supernatural sphere is not, apparently, to be seen in political changes on earth, but rather in the deliverance of individuals whose lives have been dominated by demonic power. This is not the sort of revolution many of Jesus' hearers would have been looking for. It is much more fundamental.

It would be a mistake, however, to see the overthrow of Satan merely in terms of the ministry of exorcism, however prominent this may have been. The New Testament view of Satan's activity and power ranges more widely than that, and Mark indicates as much by including two other references to Satan in a different connection. In the explanation of the parable of the sower, the birds which eat the seed sown beside the path represent Satan, who 'comes and takes away the word that is sown' (4.15); and in 8.33 Peter's total failure to understand the nature of Jesus' mission earns the extraordinary rebuke, 'Get behind me, Satan, because you do not think God's thoughts but men's thoughts.' To use the terminology of chapter 4, Peter has so far failed to grasp 'the secret of God's kingship', and his human misinterpretation of it puts him rather on the side of Satan. Satan's business, then, is to prevent the message of God's kingship from being heard and understood. It is to keep people thinking 'men's thoughts', and so to keep them insulated from God's kingship.

So a revolution against the rule of Satan is going to involve a revolution in the thinking of those who wish to come instead under God's kingship. Their minds need to be liberated from Satan's control. 'Men's thoughts' are inspired by Satan, and are the enemy of the kingdom of God. And it is that sort of revolution, the overturning of accepted human attitudes and values, which Mark's Gospel is designed to promote. He shows us the example of the disciples and other contemporaries of Jesus, who again and again found themselves challenged to rethink their basic values, and often enough failed to meet the challenge. He allows us to watch Jesus, in his ministry of compassion, brushing aside the unquestioned traditions of his society, and to listen to his revolutionary new teaching, which the Jewish authorities rightly interpreted as a threat to their inherited traditions, and even his disciples found too radical for comfort. To follow Jesus demanded a complete reorientation. The 'kingdom of God' which he preached to them proved to be, from a human perspective, an 'upside-down kingdom'.[5]

The Overturning of Human Values

Helmut Gollwitzer, or rather his translator, describes the effect of Jesus' teaching by the delightful phrase 'a bouleversement of the value scale'.[6] Its effect is summed up in a slogan which occurs more than once in the tradition of Jesus' sayings, 'Many who are first will be last, and the last first' (Mark 10.31; cf. 9.35. Also, in different contexts, Matt. 20.16; Luke 13.30). It was in this way that both his teaching and his practice came to be understood by his disciples.

They found it a difficult lesson to learn. Mark's irreverent portrayal of the disciples as dull-witted and slow to understand is often noticed, and has sometimes been seen as a deliberate vendetta with a hidden agenda (the disciples representing those whom Mark wishes to discredit in his own church context).[7] But that is to ignore the very real difficulty which Jesus' teaching must in fact have presented to those who first heard it, and to underestimate the radical nature of its challenge to existing norms. It needs no hidden agenda on the part of Mark to explain why they found it hard to cope with the reorientation which Jesus demanded – indeed it might be claimed that even two thousand years later the Church has still not fully appreciated what a revolutionary business it is to follow Jesus. For his first followers his message was no doubt exhilarating, but also frequently threatening and bewildering.

This reorientation in the disciples' thinking is highlighted particularly in the central section of Mark's Gospel which runs from 8.27 to 10.45, and which is generally and rightly regarded as focused primarily on the nature of discipleship.[8] The setting on the journey to Jerusalem ('the way', 8.27; 9.33; 10.17, 32, 52) provides a model for what it means to follow Jesus, and many have suggested that the 'framing' of the section between two accounts of the healing of blind men (8.22–6; 10.46–52), the first of which takes place only gradually, is intended to symbolize the progressive enlightenment of the disciples.[9] It is within this section of the Gospel that Jesus' three formal predictions of his passion occur (8.31; 9.31; 10.32–4), and it is remarkable that in each case the announcement of the destiny of the Son of Man is immediately followed by a response from the disciples which reveals their complete failure to come to terms with what Jesus is saying. Thus Peter rebukes Jesus for his talk of rejection and death in 8.32; and in 9.32 the disciples as a whole are unable to understand what he is talking about and are afraid to enquire, and they go on to reveal their totally different perspective by arguing about who is the greatest (9.33–4); and in 10.35–7 James and John similarly make a request which shows that they can think only of status and glory, not of rejection and suffering.

Thus Jesus' understanding of his mission has taken them entirely by surprise. But it is not only startling, it is also extremely unwelcome. To those who have understood the connotation of eschatological glory and sovereignty which is inherent in the title 'the Son of Man', this talk of being rejected by the leaders of the very people he has come to liberate, and of suffering and death as his *necessary* role, is incomprehensible. And this is not just an academic disapproval of what appears to be misguided pessimism; it has existential implications as well. To those who know Daniel's vision of the 'one like a son of man' it must seem clear that to be one of his followers is the way to glory and power; the request of James and John to share his throne was a natural sequel to being the followers of the Son of Man. The only question remaining is which of them will be the greatest among the victorious group. But now this talk of rejection and death casts an unwelcome shadow on their prospects, and they begin to wonder what they have let themselves in for. Perhaps they were afraid to ask him what he meant (9.32) not because Jesus himself as a person was too aloof and forbidding, but because they were beginning to suspect what he would say, and they did not want to hear it.

So after each of the three passion predictions, and the inept response of the disciples to it, there follows a section of teaching about discipleship which is a deliberate attempt to reorientate them to a new way of understanding the purpose of God, a new model of kingship. In 8.33 Peter's negative response to Jesus' first passion prediction (and, no doubt, his fear of what such a mission for the master must imply for the follower) earns him the epithet 'Satan', and his outlook is condemned as 'men's thoughts, not God's thoughts'. The human instinct of self-preservation is incompatible with the way of discipleship. To follow Jesus is to take up the cross, to lose one's life (8.34–7). Ultimately a choice must be made between loyalty to the Son of Man and keeping the favour of 'this adulterous and sinful generation' (8.38).

After the second passion prediction the disciples, understandably, will risk no comment! But their subsequent discussion of 'Who is the greatest?' reveals how little they have grasped the new perspective of God's kingship. So Jesus sets out the divine principle of greatness through service, of pre-eminence through being the last of all (9.35), and goes on to illustrate it by the visual aid of a child (9.36–7).

The child is actually a most effective illustration of the reversal of human value-scales, though the point is regularly obscured by preachers who try to interpret the child as a symbol of purity, innocence or receptiveness. Not only is this simply untrue to the experience of most people who have anything to do with children, but it is also irrelevant to the contexts in which Jesus uses this illustration. The point at issue is 'greatness', status, importance. And in that connection the child symbolizes the least, the lowest, the bottom of the heap. Children are dependents, minors, with no effective voice in society. They are there to be looked after and told what to do. They dream of the day when they too are grown up and have power over others, but for the moment they have to accept a position of powerlessness. Yet, as Jesus will say in another incident in the next chapter, 'To such belongs God's kingship' (10.14). In their littleness and dependency they represent the way people are meant to relate to God. And so the way you regard and respond to children is an indicator of the way you respond to Jesus and his message: 'Whoever receives one of such children in my name receives me' (9.37; cf. 10.15). To place a high value on the least is not natural; it is the mark of a value-scale which reflects that of God, in which the first are last and the last first.

The issue of status is central also in the exchange which follows the third passion prediction. James and John have heard the glorious title 'the Son of Man', the one to whom is given 'dominion and glory and kingdom, that all peoples, nations, and languages should serve him' (Dan. 7.14). That is what has appealed to their human ambition, while their minds have filtered out all that Jesus has said about the real nature of the Son of Man's mission. So Jesus explains in 10.38–40 that his glory is to be achieved by way of suffering, and that in any case positions of honour are given, not claimed. But James and John were not alone in their ambition, for I have little doubt that the 'indignation' of the other ten (v. 41) reflects not a high-minded disapproval of the brothers' carnal ambition, but annoyance that they had attempted to get in first! So Jesus' rebuke in verses 42–4 is addressed to all of them, and it focuses again on status. The desire to be top is indeed thoroughly natural: that is how society works. But 'It shall not be so among you' (v. 43). In that little clause the whole issue is summed up. To follow Jesus is to commit yourself to a way of life in which normal human rules no longer operate, to a scale of values which turns upside down the priorities by which people live and relate to one another, where the first are last and the last first.

It is the message of the child again, but this time it is reinforced with the example of Jesus himself (10.45). Again Jesus uses the pregnant title 'the Son of Man', already so incongruously linked with a mission of rejection and suffering in each of the passion predictions. It was the destiny of the 'one like a son of man' in Daniel 7 that 'all peoples, nations, and languages should serve him'; yet, says Jesus, 'the Son of Man came not to be served but to serve'. And that was the point of the apparently meaningless suffering and death which he has been predicting and which they have found it so impossible to make sense of: his service takes the form of 'giving his life as a ransom *for many*'. It is concern for others which motivates him, and leads him into a role against which every human instinct must rebel. Here surely is the ultimate 'bouleversement of the value scale'.

God's Kingship and the Way of the World – The Message of Mark 10

In the three passages which we have considered in the last section there is no explicit mention of 'the kingdom of God', and it may seem that we have strayed from our subject. But we have noted already the danger of assuming that the kingship of God is in view only where that actual phrase is used, and in fact in the last section it has never been far below the surface. Indeed there has been virtually explicit talk of kingship in James and John's hope of sitting beside Jesus in his glory, and it has been the behaviour of 'those who are thought to rule over the Gentiles' which has been used as the counterpoint to the way Jesus' followers are to behave. Human and divine ideals of kingship are being contrasted, and the revolution Jesus comes to bring is one which will overturn the authority structures of human society.

Underlying the attitude of the followers, however, is that of 'the Son of Man' himself. Jesus has taken one of the most exalted and authoritative figures of the Old Testament and has applied it to a mission which puts him on course not only for conflict with human authority, but for apparent defeat by it. The 'dominion and glory and kingdom . . . that shall not be destroyed' of Daniel 7.14 is to be fulfilled in humiliation and death. True, each of the three passion predictions also concludes with the promise of resurrection after three days, but there is no indication that the disciples even noticed this unexpected clause, still less that they understood it (cf. 9.10). The paradox of kingship through indignity and failure is what the reader, like the disciples, is likely to notice. Followers of such a king are going to stand out as different in a success-orientated society; indeed they are going to have a lot of unlearning of basic attitudes to do themselves. It is that process which we can see taking place particularly in chapter 10.

Without wishing to attribute the present chapter divisions of Mark to the original author, I find it appropriate to approach chapter 10 (with which the 'discipleship section' concludes) as a collection of incidents in which the process of re-education reaches its climax, each episode increasing the disciples' discomfort, and adding further force to the slogan which sums up the nature of discipleship, 'it shall not be so among you' (10.43). And in this chapter the phrase 'the kingdom of God' occurs prominently to designate the new perspective within which Jesus' followers must learn to operate.

The first pericope of the chapter is on divorce (10.2–12). This is not the place to go into a full discussion of the very complex exegetical issues, and the even more sensitive questions of pastoral application, which this passage raises. But I think there can be no dispute over the point which is our concern here, that Jesus' stark pronouncement rejecting the option of divorce in verse 9 was a departure from currently accepted standards which would have left many who heard him breathless. Even his disciples found it hard to take, and needed to ask him to explain himself (v. 10), though the explanation they received served only to reinforce the radical nature of his earlier pronouncement. True, there was lively debate at the time over the permitted grounds for divorce, and some rabbis were more 'rigorist' than others;[10] but even the most rigorous agreed that divorce as such was not only permissible, but was directly sanctioned by the law of God in Deuteronomy 24.1–4. And the general practice was apparently far from rigorous, if we may judge by Josephus' laconic comment, 'At this period I divorced my wife, as I was displeased at her behaviour' (*Life*, 426).[11] In refusing to sanction divorce, Jesus was thus clearly setting himself against the popular mood, and against the self-interest of the male part of his audience. But in dismissing the scriptural authority on which the permission for divorce was based he was opening up an even more controversial area, that of the right interpretation of the Word of God, and in so doing was setting himself against the whole rabbinic establishment. To follow such a teacher was clearly not going to be an easy or a popular route.

Then we have the blessing of the children (10.13–16), a passage in which we are accustomed to see the warmth and love of Jesus, and find it hard to understand how anyone could find his attitude disturbing. Yet the story is set up as one of opposition, with the disciples on the wrong side. We are not told why they objected to the children being brought, but Jesus' reply suggests that the issue was one of status. It was in that connection that he had introduced the child as a teaching aid in 9.36, and the same issue underlies this pericope. In dismissing the children as unworthy of their master's attention, the disciples reveal their failure to grasp the unconventional values of the kingdom of God. The term 'kingdom of God' is used twice in this pericope, once to say that God's kingship 'belongs to such as these', and once to say that those who wish to 'enter God's kingship' must receive it 'as a child'.[12] Those whom the disciples rejected are in fact the symbols of how divine government is exerted and experienced. The last again prove to be first.

But in 10.17 we are introduced to a potential disciple who would be a welcome recruit to any group. He is rich, earnest, and of upright character, and he is searching for 'eternal life'. The disciples have been going out to catch such fish for Jesus, but here is one leaping into the net of his own accord! But Jesus seems to go out of his way to repel the man. He questions the theology of his polite form of address (v. 18), and goes on to put before him such an unreasonable demand that the enquirer goes away hurt and crestfallen. The disciples can hardly believe it. Their 'extreme astonishment' (vv. 24, 26) is summed up in the words, 'Then who can be saved?' If this man cannot be enrolled as a disciple, who else could possibly qualify? But the problem lies in precisely the area which from the human point of view makes him such an attractive catch, his affluence. The rabbis in general understood wealth as a token of God's blessing,[13] but here again Jesus reverses accepted values. Wealth is an impediment, indeed so grave an impediment that rich people *cannot* enter God's kingship. It is not just 'difficult' (vv. 23, 24), for Jesus goes on to say that the total impossibility of getting a camel through the eye of a needle[14] is easier than getting a rich man into the kingdom of God (v. 25). The disciples' reaction, 'Then who can be saved?', was entirely justified. That *was* what Jesus meant, as he goes on to confirm in verse 27: humanly speaking it *is* impossible.

But that is just the point. The whole discussion has assumed a *human* perspective. The human valuation which made this man such an attractive recruit is worthless from the point of view of God's kingship. As verse 27 goes on to say, salvation *is* possible, but not on human terms. It is a divine miracle. To approach the kingship of God on any other basis is to miss the point. Perhaps that is why Mark has included the phrase 'the kingdom of God' three times in this short dialogue. The disciples' astonishment (and disapproval?) at Jesus' treatment of the rich man revealed that they had not yet begun to weigh things up from the perspective of *divine* government.

But at least affluence had not kept *them* from responding to Jesus' call, and Peter says as much with more than a hint of smug self-congratulation (v. 28). Yet even here there are new attitudes to be learned, for while Jesus acknowledges the principle that God is no man's debtor and that sacrifices accepted for the sake of Jesus and his mission will be amply compensated, there is a sting in the tail of the list of earthly recompense in that these things come 'with persecutions' (v. 30). The call to lose one's life in following Jesus which has been sounded in 8.34–8 is here modified, perhaps, by the mention of earthly compensation, but it is certainly not rescinded. To follow Jesus is still to opt for the way of persecution.

It is at this point that Mark includes the slogan 'There will be many who are first who will be last, and the last first' (10.31), which so well summarizes the reversal of values which Jesus is teaching, and which could so appropriately have followed either the story of blessing the children or that of the rich man. But why does it occur just here, after Peter's comment about leaving everything to follow

Jesus? Is it merely an observation arising out of Jesus' reply, that those who seemed to have made themselves last by their sacrifice turn out in fact to be first in the recompense they receive, while those who seemed to have kept everything will, in their failure to attain everlasting life, prove to be the eventual losers?

Perhaps it is no more than that, but it is introduced by the conjunction *de*, which is normally translated by 'but', and suggests a *contrast* with what preceded, or at least a change of focus, rather than a simple continuation of the same idea. Admittedly, *de* is a very common and not always clearly marked particle, and it would be hazardous to base any exegesis on the assumption that it *must* imply contrast. But at this point several commentators are prepared at least to entertain the possibility that verse 31 adds a note of warning to the disciples.[15] Is there a sense of complacency in Peter's proclamation of the sacrifice the disciples have made, perhaps even the assumption that this sacrifice has in some way 'earned' the eternal life which the rich man lost through his failure to give up his wealth? But there can be no automatic front-rank status even for those who have given up most. And perhaps verse 31 is in fact directed more specifically against Peter himself. Did his unsolicited outburst in verse 28 betray a sense of superiority, even a claim to leadership, as the first to have given everything up to follow Jesus (1.16–18)? Such an interpretation of verse 31 would offer an appropriate basis for the sequel in verses 35–7, where James and John (the other two members of the 'inner circle' of three: 5.37; 9.2; 14.33; cf. 1.16–20, 29; 13.3) try to profit by Peter's temporary eclipse by staking their own claim to pre-eminence.

It is this theme of leadership and ambition which dominates the following section arising out of Jesus' third passion prediction (10.32–45). We have already considered that passage earlier in this chapter, and need not here repeat its warning against following the world's ideas of greatness, summarized in the slogan, 'It shall not be so among you' (10.43).

So even within the new situation of God's kingship into which Jesus has brought his disciples they must beware of letting human attitudes and conventions control their thinking. God's reversal of values operates within the disciple community as well as unseating those outside. It is not the natural leader who takes precedence, but rather, as in Isaiah's vision of God's holy mountain, 'a little child shall lead them' (Isa. 11.6).

Jesus the Radical

Mark's Jesus shocked people, and seems not have minded doing so! Our study of chapter 10 has revealed how uncomfortable his own followers found both his teaching and his activity. His challenges to their basic value-scale, together with his paradoxical vision of the mission which he himself must fulfil as 'the Son of Man', left them bewildered and uneasy.

Mark captures this mood vividly in the little cameo which introduces the third passion prediction. The journey to Jerusalem has already begun, and Jesus has made no secret of what he expects to happen when they get there; indeed, his rejection and death is apparently the very purpose of the journey. In that context,

> They were on the road, going up to Jerusalem; Jesus himself was forging ahead of them, and the disciples were astounded, while those who followed were frightened. (10.32)

Mark's word for the disciples' astonishment is a strong one: one might say that they were dazed, even shell-shocked! The determined march to death simply didn't make sense, and they wished they were not there.

If his disciples found Jesus hard to take, it is not surprising that others were shocked by him. The opposition to Jesus which is so consistent a feature of the narrative development of Mark's Gospel reflects this inability to come to terms with the values on which he operated. His apparently cavalier attitude to the conventions of Jewish society and religion inevitably made him enemies. He was, in other words, a dangerous radical.

In matters of *halakah* (the rabbinic term for rules formulated to govern behaviour) he had a disconcerting way of cutting through generations of carefully spun debate and exhaustively formulated

rules of conduct by introducing far-reaching principles and questions
of priority. We have seen an example in his teaching on divorce,
where the careful rabbinic debate on the precise application of
Deuteronomy 24.1–4 is set aside by Jesus' appeal to an earlier, and
in his view more fundamental, principle in the law, that of man and
woman becoming one flesh (Gen. 1.27 and 2.24, as quoted in Mark
10.6–8). If that was God's purpose for marriage, the whole debate
on divorce becomes unnecessary, for what was merely a concession
to deal with human weakness ('for the hardness of your hearts',
10.5) can never be the basis for determining the standard God really
requires.

Even more threatening to accepted patterns of conduct was Jesus'
attitude to the issue of ritual purity, a matter sufficiently important
in rabbinic debate to be the subject of the whole of one of the six
tractates of the Mishnah (*Tohoroth*, the sixth tractate). Mark devotes
one of his longest sections of teaching-cum-dialogue (7.1–23) to a
debate on the subject, initiated by scribes from Jerusalem who
objected to the failure of Jesus' disciples to observe strict laws of
purity. The particular issue which they raised (that of washing
hands before meals) was not one on which the Old Testament
offered direct guidance, though the current *halakah* could be
defended as an extension to ordinary life of the Old Testament
principle of cultic purity for priests (e.g. Exod. 30.18–21). But
Jesus, rather than disputing the validity of this extension of the law
(and he might well have found substantial support for such a
query),[16] first launches into an apparently gratuitous attack, unrelated
to the washing issue, on the scribes' way of evading the demands of
the law by means of conveniently formulated *halakah* (vv. 6–13),
but then goes on to undercut the whole principle of cultic purity by
his all-embracing pronouncement that it is not what goes into a
person which defiles them, but what comes out (v. 15). Mark rightly
describes this as a 'parable' (v. 17), an epigrammatic saying which
does not constitute a direct abrogation of the Old Testament laws of
purity, but he then goes on to interpret it in an editorial comment in
verse 19 as 'declaring all foods clean', and few would doubt that this
is a proper deduction from Jesus' parable. It was on this basis that
the growing Church quickly emancipated itself from the Jewish
food laws.

Yet this was not just an attack on scribal *halakah*, but on a principle of the Mosaic law (even though Jesus has just accused the scribes of undermining the authority of that same law by their traditions!). And unlike the dismissal of Deuteronomy 24.1–4 as a basis for divorce, this pronouncement was not supported by an alternative text from the Old Testament, but merely by Jesus' sovereign pronouncement on what constitutes true defilement. This is probably the most extreme example in Mark (and indeed in all the Gospels) of the 'radicalism' which made Jesus' preaching anathema to the scribal establishment. But there were plenty of other examples, supremely his dismissal of generations of sabbath *halakah* on the basis of the dangerously elastic principles that the sabbath was made for man, not man for the sabbath (2.27), and that it is right to do good on the sabbath (3.4)!

But Jesus sat loose to strict observance of the laws of purity not only in his teaching but also in practice. Prominent in the Gospels as a cause of offence was his habit of moving in undesirable company, that of 'tax-collectors and sinners', and, even worse, of eating meals with them. This was not only an offence against ritual purity,[17] but also against Jewish national sentiment, since tax-collectors in particular were professionally identified with the Roman occupation. Mark records this behaviour of Jesus as a major scandal to 'the scribes of the Pharisees' (2.15–17), and anyone who shared the patriotic view of tax-collectors as quislings must have been equally horrified. Yet clearly this was no temporary lapse by Jesus, but a matter of settled policy, a deliberate challenge to the 'exclusivist' approach to what it means to be the people of God which was held by the scribal establishment.[18] God's kingship is open not only to the ritually pure, but to the outcast and disreputable. Ben Meyer rightly understands Jesus' proclamation of God's kingship as characterized by the theme of 'gratuity', 'salvation as free gift',[19] though he does not go so far as E. P. Sanders in suggesting that Jesus dispensed even with the need for repentance, and welcomed 'sinners' without requiring any change of life (a suggestion which has not convinced many!).[20]

Thus Jesus, as Mark portrays him, not only challenged his own disciples to rethink their accepted values and attitudes, but also confronted several of the basic principles on which Jewish society operated and aimed to turn these also upside down. Even the clearly scriptural principle of ritual purity was not exempt from this searching critique, and subsequent rabbinic development of *halakah* was treated with a lack of respect which inevitably turned the religious establishment against him.

All this goes to support the proposal that Jesus' language about the kingdom of God could be paraphrased in terms of 'revolution'. The institution of divine government is going to have radical results, and the values and principles on which human society operates, even among the people of God, are going to be turned upside down. The last will be first, and the first last.

What Sort of Revolution?

Jesus' radicalism might seem, then, to make him a natural ally of the Zealots, whose programme included not only liberation from Roman imperialism, but also the reform of social and economic abuses within the Jewish community.[21] The language of 'overthrow', 'reversal', 'turning upside down' which we have been using is the language of socio-political revolution, and there is little doubt that both Jesus' attitude to existing social distinctions and his radical teaching encouraged many of his followers to expect his movement to lead to dramatic changes in the social and political structures in which they lived.

There is one pericope in Mark where the issue of Jesus' attitude to militant nationalism is directly raised. The question about paying taxes to Caesar (12.13–17) focused on the specific issue which had been the flash-point of the revolt of Judas of Galilee a generation earlier, and which remained at the root of the Zealot ideology: the people of God must not acknowledge a human master, since God is their king, and Roman taxation is a symbol of such submission.[22] Jesus' reply, 'Return to Caesar what is Caesar's and to God what is God's', is often interpreted as merely a clever evasion of a trick question. But while it does serve admirably to extricate Jesus from a tight corner, it is by no means empty of content. Whereas a Zealot must see Caesar and God as all-out rivals, Jesus' words accept that each has a legitimate claim, in other words that human and divine government are not in principle incompatible. How their claims relate to one another, and what one must do when they come into conflict, Jesus does not say. But he takes it for granted that such conflict is not inevitable.

So Jesus is not a Zealot. He is not launching a movement dedicated to the overthrow of socio-political structures. Even the government of the people of God by the imperial power of Rome seems in principle acceptable to him, however carefully it must be qualified in the light of the need to bring to God what is God's. When it comes to taking direct action, it begins to look as if the radicalism of Jesus is dissolved into a tame acceptance of the status quo. So what has happened to the 'revolution' he proclaimed, if divine government leaves the structures of human society untouched?

Mark does not offer any hint of a specific reform programme which Jesus espoused, nor do the other Gospels add anything to Mark in this respect. Few have been convinced by the proposal, on the basis of Luke 4.18–21, that Jesus was campaigning for the redistribution of wealth and the freeing of slaves by means of a literal implementation of the Old Testament jubilee regulations.[23] Other attempts to claim Jesus' support for specific programmes of socio-political action have been no more successful. While Jesus had a great deal to say about social divisions and inequality in areas such as race, class and wealth, and showed his concern by his own uninhibited behaviour in relation to the barriers set up by convention, he offered his followers no blueprint for the righting of all wrongs and did not himself, as far as our records go, produce any manifesto for social reform.[24]

What Jesus did call for was, as we have seen, a revolution of values, and such revolutions must begin at the level of personal transformation rather than with the change of social or political systems. It was as people were 'given' the knowledge of the secret of God's kingship that they began to see with new eyes. Even so, it was a gradual and often painful process of reorientation, as Mark's 'discipleship section' vividly illustrates.

So it is not surprising that Jesus' first announcement of divine government in Mark 1.15 involves a call for personal change. 'Repent' carries for English readers a rather restrictive connotation of spiritual grief and penance. But *metanoeite* says much more than that. It is a call for transformation, for reorientation, for a new beginning in a direction contrary to that of a person's former life, for a new life under God's kingship. It is this new beginning which is in view also when Jesus speaks elsewhere about 'entering God's kingship' (9.47; 10.23–5). It is to begin a new relationship with God, as a subject of his rule. 'To enter God's kingship' in 9.47 stands in parallel with 'to enter into life' in 9.43 and 9.45, while the alternative in each of these verses is to be thrown into Gehenna. And in 10.26 the verb 'to be saved' is placed in parallel with 'to enter God's kingship' in the preceding three verses. To enter God's kingship is therefore a total transformation, with effects reaching beyond life on earth to a person's eternal destiny. It is the beginning of life with God. And that makes everything different.

But the personal change of values which Jesus required must obviously have an effect on the lifestyle and relationships of those who followed him. The new relationship with God into which they had entered could never be a purely private, individual affair, and it is particularly in their relations with one another that the new values of God's kingship must begin to operate. Hence the frequent stress on matters of status and leadership, the call to welcome the insignificant, and to serve rather than be served. The slogan 'It shall not be so among you' (10.43) points not so much to distinctive individuals as to a transformed community, an alternative society in conscious contrast with the way of the world. In this topsy-turvy community, where the first are last and the last first, the new values of divine government can begin to take visible form.

And when that happens, as a result of the inward transformation which God's kingship demands, there is the promise of a *truly* transformed society, not changed merely by a reordering of its structures, but by a reorientation of its values. That is the truly revolutionary change which Jesus came to bring, and which Mark's emphasis on the re-education of the disciples holds constantly before his readers. When such a transformation occurs within a group of people, the kingship of God becomes real on earth as it is in heaven. And such an alternative community will inevitably have its effect on the life and the values of the rest of society, not so much by campaigning for a predetermined blueprint of reform to be implemented, but by bringing the revolutionary values of divine government to bear on the context in which they find themselves in whatever way may best suit that particular situation.

To recognize this perspective on God's kingship is not to settle for a cosy pietism which leaves social and political reform to become the province of those who do not share God's values. No one who has even begun to think 'God's thoughts' could be content with such an abdication of responsibility for God's world. Those who have learned to see the selfishness and inequality of human society as Jesus saw it will share his anger and will be as eager as he was to break down barriers and to exercise his compassion towards the disadvantaged, not only individually but corporately. It is the kingship of God which will inspire this concern and will guide their search for appropriate ways to put it into action. But neither Jesus' example nor his teaching offer any single universally applicable practical panacea for the ills of society, even though they provide both the motivation and the scale of values without which no effective change can be expected.

That is why those who have tried to define the kingdom of God in terms of a particular social or political system have so often been disappointed. It is too radical to allow such human systematization. It places every human system beneath the critical scrutiny of the revolutionary values of God himself. And so it brings about a transformation of human life from within, in a way no human revolution could ever do, precisely because it is *God's* revolution.

4

Government and Power

I recently received a piece of 'crank-mail' proving irrefutably that Christianity is wrong. Its focus was on the clear teaching of Jesus in Mark 9.1 that the kingdom of God would have arrived within the lifetime of some of his contemporaries; it did not, so Jesus was wrong, and the whole of Christianity is founded on a man whose word could not be trusted. Few Christians can fail at some time to have been embarrassed by this simple equation, whether directed at them by sceptical non-Christians or arising out of their own reading of the New Testament. Several times the note of imminence recurs, and on a number of occasions it is linked to specific time-clauses limiting the fulfilment of Jesus' words to the then current generation.

Three passages in Mark's Gospel pose this problem in rather different ways.

Mark 9.1:   Truly I say to you, there are some of those standing here who will by no means taste death until they see the kingdom of God having come with power.

Mark 13.30: Truly I say to you, this generation will by no means pass away until all these things have happened

(and 'all these things' appear on a straightforward reading to include 'the Son of Man coming on the clouds with great power and glory' and the sending out of the angels to gather in the chosen).

Mark 14.62: *You* will see the Son of Man sitting on the right hand of Power and coming with the clouds of heaven.

A further similarly time-bound prediction in Matthew 10.23 ('You will not have completed all the towns of Israel before the Son of Man comes') does not occur in Mark, but clearly operates within a similar field of language and ideas.

While these sayings are widely separated in Mark's Gospel, it seems legitimate to treat them together in view of the fact that the same motifs recur. The Son of Man is the central figure in 13.26 and 14.62, and has been so also in the verse which leads into 9.1, which speaks of the Son of Man coming in the glory of his Father with the holy angels (8.38). All three passages envisage kingship or enthronement in one way or another (even though the actual phrase 'the kingdom of God' occurs only in 9.1), and the association of this idea with references to the Son of Man suggests that the enthronement of the 'one like a son of man' in Daniel 7.13–14 is the inspiration behind their formulation; references to glory, power, clouds and angels add to this impression of the dominant influence of Daniel's vision. All three passages specifically mention 'power' (*dynamis*). All refer to people being able to *see* this power in operation, and all locate that seeing within the living generation (assuming that the 'you' of 14.62 is intended to refer to Jesus' judges in the Sanhedrin, as surely must be indicated by the dramatic reversal of roles which Jesus' saying predicts).[1]

Moreover, all three passages are marked as significant pronouncements: the first two are introduced by the solemn formula '*Amen* I say to you', while the third occurs in a place of special prominence as Jesus' climactic self-declaration (after long silence) before the supreme court of the people of God, the moment when the 'messianic secret' is at last publicly divulged. So these are not incidental, ill-considered comments, but solemn declarations of Jesus' vision for the fulfilment of God's purpose through his mission as the Son of Man.

These are clearly key passages for understanding Mark's view of the kingdom of God. All of them link the ideas of kingship and of power. And all of them are clearly relevant to the temporal question already raised by Mark 1.15, 'The kingdom of God has drawn near . . .' If that passage left room for doubt as to when exactly the time of fulfilment was understood to be (though, as I have shown above (pp. 23–5), there seems little room for doubt in view of the preceding clause, 'the time has been fulfilled'!), these three passages all make clearly temporal statements which rule out any idea that

Jesus was talking merely about the implementation of God's kingship at some indefinite time in the future.

In this chapter a substantial amount of space will be devoted to discussing Mark 9.1, since this is a key text for understanding Jesus' expectation.[2] But I believe that a proper understanding of this passage will give us important perspectives for the other passages I have mentioned, and indeed for that whole area of Jesus' teaching which is concerned with the working out of God's purpose, the effective implementation of his kingship.

Mark 9.1 – 'Seeing the Kingdom of God Having Come with Power'

In the above heading I have pedantically translated the Greek by 'having come' in order to make it clear that whereas Mark 13.26 and 14.62 speak of seeing the Son of Man 'coming' (using the same present form of the verb as Theodotion's Greek version of Dan. 7.13), Mark 9.1 has a perfect participle, 'having come', which in normal usage implies that the coming has preceded the seeing. So according to Mark Jesus solemnly declares that while some of those standing there are still alive the kingdom of God will have come with power.

The parallel sayings in Matthew and Luke are interestingly different. In Matthew this saying is more closely tied up with the preceding verse (from which it is separated in Mark by the transition formula, 'And he was saying to them'). Matthew 16.27 speaks of the Son of Man coming in glory as judge, accompanied by the angels, and 16.28 goes on to declare that some of those present will not taste death until they see 'the Son of Man coming in his kingship'. The coming of the kingship of God in power is thus personalized as the coming of the Son of Man as king as well as judge. But it is still a visible 'coming'. In Luke 9.27, on the other hand, as in Mark 9.1, there is no mention of the Son of Man to pick up that in the preceding verse, but what the bystanders will see is expressed merely as 'the kingdom of God' – no 'coming', no 'power', merely 'seeing the kingdom of God', a phrase which can more easily be interpreted of a general perception of God's work in the world, and less specifically of a visible 'coming'; probably Luke so intended it, since his parallel to Mark 14.62 has similarly removed both the 'seeing' and the 'coming', leaving only the fact of the Son of Man sitting at the right hand of the power of God (Luke 22.69).

Luke, then, perhaps reveals some embarrassment over the apparent suggestion that a visible event was to be expected within the lifetime of Jesus' contemporaries which has not in fact occurred by the time of his writing. Mark and Matthew have no such inhibitions. They phrase the nature of the 'coming' differently, but each is quite clear that 'some of those standing here' will see it before they die.[3]

The phrase 'will by no means taste death until' is generally treated as simply a way of expressing the time limit of the present generation, but the wording is surprising, both in the emphatic *ou me,* 'by no means', and in the language of 'tasting death' rather than 'dying'. If 9.1 is treated merely as an isolated logion, divorced from its preceding context, this seems strangely heavy language to refer to the current generation. But seen in the light of the preceding verses these terms make more sense. For Jesus has just been talking about death, not just his own (8.31), but that of those who follow him (8.34-7). And this is not death through old age, but martyrdom; it is, for them as for him, a cross deliberately taken up, a 'loss of life' knowingly accepted 'for my sake and the gospel's'. Such a 'tasting of death' may well be the lot of those who choose not to be ashamed of Jesus in the face of 'this adulterous and sinful generation' (8.38). And it might then seem that 'this generation' has prevailed over the Son of Man. But there is an alternative society, another generation of those already standing here, who, unlike some of their fellow disciples, will *by no means* suffer martyrdom until they have seen the fulfilment of what they have stood for. The emphatic *ou me* points to the certainty of the victory of the Son of Man over the opposition of 'this generation', improbable as it may have seemed to those who in the meantime have had to 'taste death' for his sake and the gospel's.[4]

To recognize that the emphatic language about 'by no means tasting death' is accounted for by the preceding context does not, however, in the least reduce the temporal limitation placed on the coming of the kingdom of God with power. People currently alive will see it before they die. But is this 'seeing' placed in the future because the coming of God's kingship is to be expected some time between Jesus' saying these words and the end of their lives, or will they become aware in the future of something which has *already* been there for those with eyes to see it? If we were right in interpreting Mark 1.15 as a statement of the *arrival*, not merely the *imminence*, of divine government, the latter would seem to be the case; the kingdom of God has already come in the ministry of Jesus, and anyone could already at that time see it as 'having come' (perfect tense). Yet Jesus' words here clearly point to the future: they 'will not taste death until . . .' It does not sound as if he is describing the status quo.

The solution to this problem seems to me to lie in the concept of hidden growth which we examined in Chapter Two. The seed is planted and growing, but the mature plant is not yet visible. God's kingship is operative, but in secret, unobserved by most people. It has come indeed, but it has not yet visibly come *with power.* That last phrase moves us away from a rigid temporal scheme in which at one moment there is no kingship of God and at the next there it is complete. There is a process of development, a process which Jesus has set in motion, as his declaration in Mark 1.15 makes clear, but which must increasingly work itself out from hiddenness and weakness to visibility and power.

It is this process of growth which also offers the clue to the problem from which we began. Those who claim that Jesus' pronouncement in Mark 9.1 was self-evidently mistaken do so on the basis of a particular understanding of what period or event Jesus was referring to when he spoke of 'God's kingship having come with power'. It seems often to be taken for granted that he was speaking of his parousia and of the end of the world, yet there is remarkably little in Mark 9.1 to suggest any such idea. The parousia reference is presumably introduced into 9.1 on the basis of the language about 'the Son of Man coming' in 8.38 (and of Matthew's different version of the saying which envisages 'the Son of Man coming in his kingship', 16.28). Later in the chapter we shall return to the issue of what is meant by these references to Daniel 7.13, the 'coming of one like a son of man', and I shall argue there (pp. 73–82) that this is not in the first place parousia language. But in any case this is not the language Mark 9.1 uses; it speaks rather of the powerful coming of God's kingship. The question as to what specific event or situation Jesus intended such language to refer to, and when it may have happened, remains to be answered – and it remains open to question whether a proper exegesis of Mark 9.1 requires us to settle for one particular event or situation at all. The history of its exegesis suggests that the answer to this question may not be so self-evident as some have imagined.

Has Mark 9.1 Been Fulfilled? If so, When?

Specific proposals for the intended reference for the phrase 'God's kingship having come with power' include the following:

1. The death of Jesus, seen as the 'day of the Lord', when the establishment of God's rule was powerfully shown by the torn curtain of the temple, and the centurion *saw* the truth about Jesus.[5]
2. The resurrection, the visible, powerful proof of the triumph of God over all opposition.
3. The ascension, when Jesus visibly went to take up his seat at the right hand of divine power.
4. Pentecost, when the Church 'received power' to continue Jesus' mission through the coming of the Spirit.
5. The powerful development of the Church in the early years after Pentecost, as the new dynamic of the Spirit's coming produced ever more widely visible evidence that a new day had dawned.
6. The destruction of the temple in AD 70, seen as the symbol of the end of the old order and the powerful vindication of the Son of Man whom the Jewish authorities had attempted to destroy.[6]

All these events or phases of development were in some sense *visible* to at least some observers, and all did in fact occur within the lifetime of some of those who were listening to Jesus in Mark 9.1. No doubt that is why they have commended themselves to interpreters who do not wish gratuitously to attribute a false statement to Jesus. But when so many 'rival' identifications of 'the coming of the kingdom of God with power' are offered, without any widely convincing reason to prefer one of them to the others, we do well to be cautious before committing ourselves to any one of them.

After all, Mark does not talk about the occurrence of an *event*, leaving us to guess what event it might be, but rather about seeing that God's kingship has come with power. Any or all of the above occurrences did in one way or another reveal this truth. The hiddenness of Jesus' mission during the days of his earthly ministry was already being opened up even before the cross, in his open declaration of his role as Messiah and Son of Man to the supreme court of Israel in Mark 14.62, and while his situation at that time was conspicuously lacking in 'power', his words pointed forward precisely to the reversal of that situation when he would be seen seated 'at the right hand of Power'. Those who saw the tearing of the temple curtain may already have begun to get the message, and those who heard of his resurrection had at least the opportunity to recognize that his words were coming true. The ascension was, of course, a private event, though seen by some (most?) of those who had heard his words in Mark 9.1. But subsequent events made it ever more publicly obvious that the tables had been turned, and that the hidden inauguration of God's kingship was working itself out in power. So where could one 'see the kingdom of God having come with power'? In any or all of these occurrences, depending on whether you had eyes to see what was going on. At first the truth was clear only to the few to whom 'the secret of the kingship of God' had been given, but as events progressed it became increasingly difficult for any but the completely obdurate observer to deny that there was divine power at work in the movement which had emerged from the 'weakness' of Jesus' hidden mission.

But of course none of these occurrences *is* in itself the coming of the kingdom of God with power. All witness to it, and all offer to those who see them the opportunity to recognize the truth about God's kingship. But God's kingship, as we saw in Chapter One, can never be tied down to one specific event or situation. So Mark 9.1 should not be interpreted as a prediction of any one specific event, but of the new situation of the powerful implementation of divine government which would in many ways become visible before 'some of those standing here' faced the martyrdom to which their following of Jesus committed them.

'After Six Days'

So far we have considered Mark 9.1 in relation to its preceding context (though we have not yet looked fully at the implications of the language used in 8.38), but have ignored what is in fact a striking link with the following pericope. Temporal links between events in Mark's story (outside the passion narrative) tend to be unspecific. New incidents are introduced often by such phrases as 'and immediately', 'and again', and even more commonly by a simple 'and', or 'and it happened'. So the precise notice 'and after six days' with which 9.2 begins stands out as an unusual temporal link. While it is likely that Mark was interested in the symbolism of the period of 'six days', which serves to link the following transfiguration story to its Old Testament background,[7] it is also probable that he intends the reader to notice the careful temporal link for its own sake, and to draw the conclusion that the sequence of events here is important. E. Best, arguing that the 'six days' belongs to the tradition, while Mark 9.1 owes its presence here to Mark's editorial hand, sees the link as being not with the *sayings* which conclude with 9.1, but with the latest section of narrative, the Caesarea Philippi incident.[8] But the fact remains that in the final text of Mark a temporal prediction ('some of those standing here will not taste death until . . .') is immediately followed by an unusually precise temporal link ('And after six days . . .'), and there seems no reason to assume that this happened by accident, and that Mark was unaware of the effect produced.[9]

This interpretation is regularly met by the objection that the grandiloquent language of 9.1 ('some of those standing here will by no means taste death until they have seen . . .') is an odd way of referring to an event which will occur the next week! C. K. Barrett is typical: 'if Jesus solemnly affirmed that some at least of his hearers would survive his prediction by one week he was uttering ridiculous bathos'.[10] But it must be remembered that it *was* only *some* of Jesus' hearers who were allowed to accompany him up the 'high mountain', and that Mark stresses this point by adding the phrase *kat' idian monous* to underline their privilege over against the others. The rest of those who were with Jesus at Caesarea

Philippi *did* taste death without seeing what Peter, James and John saw the following week – and it was not the sort of thing most mortal eyes can ever expect to see. The language of 9.1 does not seem to me at all inappropriate for a heavenly vision granted to a privileged few while on earth, but not to others before they die.

A more serious objection to understanding Mark 9.1 as fulfilled in the transfiguration lies in the nature of the event itself. In what sense can a private vision shared by three bewildered men be understood as a demonstration of God's kingship 'in power'? The transfiguration, for all its powerful symbolism, did not in fact introduce a dramatic change in the earthly fortunes of the preaching of God's kingship. Hiddenness, paradox, misunderstanding and weakness remain the marks of Jesus' ministry and of his disciples' experience. 'Power' still seems to be reserved for a future period. The effect of the transfiguration was to give the three chosen disciples a glimpse behind the scenes, not unlike that which Mark has given to his readers in his prologue. They will now be in a position to assess what is going on around them against a broader background, and to remember, even as the Son of Man goes to rejection and death in Jerusalem, that he is also the Son of God whose true glory has for a few minutes dazzled them. But the power and the glory remain at the level of vision.

And yet what Jesus promised in Mark 9.1 was itself at the level of vision: 'some of those standing here *will see* . . .' To see Jesus conversing with the eschatological figures Elijah and Moses,[11] to see his other-worldly splendour, and to hear him described by the voice of God himself as his beloved Son, and the one to whom attention must now be given (an echo of the expectation of the coming prophet like Moses in Deut. 18.15), was to be shown, even before the event, that the day of God's eschatological salvation has come. As yet, most could not see it, but to these three the vision was given to show that divine government had already been established in the coming of Jesus.

But of course, as virtually all commentators agree, that is not *all* that Mark 9.1 refers to. What was given in advance to the three disciples on the mountain would be given progressively to other disciples and eventually to the whole world, as divine government became ever more visible through the acts of power which were to follow once Jesus' destiny of suffering and death was completed. If indeed Mark did intend us to see the transfiguration story as *a* fulfilment of Jesus' words in 9.1, the words 'in power' prevent us from seeing it as *the* fulfilment. It was a proleptic vision of a reality which was still to be worked out in human experience.

I suspect that a lot of our problems in understanding biblical predictions stem from our unwillingness to recognize that fulfilment may be a *process* rather than a single event. It is tidier to be able to link each biblical prediction with a specific event or time when it is fulfilled, and often this is exegetically responsible. But not always. There is an element of continuity, and of escalation, about the way God works out his purpose within biblical history which requires us to look for repeated patterns, for stages of fulfilment. This is, of course, the principle that underlies biblical typology, but a similar element of progressive fulfilment applies also to much biblical prediction. We shall be considering this in relation to Daniel 7.13-14 later in this chapter, but here it is important to recognize that the expectation of the coming of God's kingship is a clear case, perhaps even the paradigm case, of progressive fulfilment. To proclaim, as Jesus clearly did, that the kingdom of God has come is not to say that there is nothing further to be expected. And to predict that some of those then living would see the kingdom of God having come with power is not necessarily to speak of a particular event, whether the transfiguration, the resurrection, Pentecost, or the parousia. It is simply to say that within the lifetime of some of those present the process of implementation of divine government will have progressed so far and so powerfully that its reality will be undeniable for those with eyes to see it. The mustard seed, which has already begun its secret growth, will have become by then a visible and impressive plant.

The Coming of the Son of Man

I hope that we have spent enough time on the exegesis of Mark 9.1 to see how little basis there is in that verse for the simplistic argument from which we began, that Jesus predicted his parousia

within the current generation, and that he was wrong. As far as
Mark 9.1 is concerned the argument could hardly be more perverse,
since that verse makes no mention of the parousia, and there is
nothing in its wording to suggest that any such idea is in mind.

But of course Mark 9.1 does not stand alone. We have seen that
the parallel in Matthew 16.28 predicts that 'some of those standing
here will by no means taste death until they see the Son of Man
coming in his kingship'. Moreover, Mark 9.1 itself is preceded by a
statement about the Son of Man coming in the glory of his Father
with the holy angels, and two further passages in Mark, 13.26 and
14.62, use similar language about a coming of the Son of Man
which is in the one case explicitly (13.30) and in the other implicitly
set within the same time-scale as Mark 9.1. To claim that Mark 9.1
does not in itself mention an imminent parousia may then seem a
rather hollow victory when it is surrounded on all sides by other
texts which seem to demand such an interpretation. It is not only the
coming of God's kingship in power which will be visible within the
generation, but also the coming of the Son of Man.

Our study is of Mark, and so I beg leave not to use space here
discussing Matthew 16.28 (and the peculiarly Matthean passage,
10.23, which raises the same issue). I hope that the conclusions I
shall draw from the Mark passages will prove relevant also to these
texts in Matthew, and shall attempt to indicate briefly before the end
of the chapter how that may be so. But for the moment I must
concentrate on Mark.

The three passages about the future 'coming of the Son of Man' in
Mark are all clearly based on Daniel 7.13–14. The mere fact that
they all use the title 'the Son of Man' does not in itself prove a
conscious allusion to Daniel 7.13, since, while I have no doubt that
it was from that passage that Jesus developed his chosen title for
himself, he clearly went on to use that title in many different
contexts where there is no discernible link with Daniel 7.[12] But all
three passages refer also to his 'coming' (which is the one active verb
associated with the human figure of Dan. 7.13), and each picks up
aspects of the heavenly imagery of the Daniel scene (in Mark 8.38
glory, a retinue of holy angels, and a context of judgement; in Mark
13.26 coming in the clouds with power and glory, and sending out
the angels; in Mark 14.62 coming with the clouds of heaven and

sitting beside the throne of God). In order to understand these passages, therefore, it is important to take into account the meaning of the language in Daniel on which they are modelled.

The focus of much of the book of Daniel, and of the vision of chapter 7 in particular, is, as we have seen in Chapter One, on kingship (pp. 17–18). Chapter 7 is about the destruction of rival empires, and their replacement by the sovereignty of 'the people of the saints of the Most High' (7.27). After the introduction of the four beasts who symbolize the pagan empires (or, more specifically, 'four kings', 7.17), the scene shifts to the throne of God himself. He sits as judge in dazzling splendour, surrounded by his heavenly court, and the temporary power and sovereignty of the four beasts is brought to an end. It is in this context of heavenly glory and judgement that Daniel sees a human figure, 'one like a son of man', coming in the clouds of heaven, coming to the throne of God, and presented before him; the sovereignty which the beasts had usurped is given to him, and his rule will be universal and unending. This, then, is a vision of enthronement. The true and eternal king is being installed beside the throne of God.

This is the language which lies behind Jesus' words in Mark 8.38, 13.26 and 14.62. It is the language of enthronement, not of parousia. The scene is in heaven, and the 'coming' of the 'one like a son of man' is to God on his heavenly throne, not to the earth. The verb 'to come' refers to his presentation before the throne, not to a 'descent' to earth. It is of course possible that Jesus might take these words of Daniel and apply them in a sense quite alien to their Old Testament context, to talk about his return from heaven to earth instead of his triumphant enthronement in heaven. But such a radical change of scene would need to be clearly signalled if he was not to be seriously misunderstood by those to whom the language of Daniel was already familiar. Unless the New Testament context clearly indicates otherwise, language about the 'coming of the Son of Man' must be assumed to refer to enthronement, to the inauguration of his kingship. And as we shall see, in each case in Mark the context not only allows but strongly encourages such an understanding. This is not the language of parousia.

That sounds a strangely paradoxical claim to modern Christian ears. To us it is axiomatic that 'the coming of the Son of Man' is one of several ways in which the New Testament describes Jesus' future return to earth. From a very early stage in the Church's history this Danielic language was generally understood in that sense (though there remained a number among patristic writers who continued to apply it rather to Jesus' enthronement).[13] And so it is natural for us to read back this later Christian usage and to assume that Jesus used it in the same sense. I would question, however, whether that is legitimate, and would like to suggest that when a usage of Daniel's language which respects its original sense is appropriate to the contexts in which Jesus uses it, the burden of proof must be on those who wish to take it in any other sense.

I am not suggesting, of course, that there is a complete divorce between the ideas of Jesus' enthronement and his parousia. The subsequent shift in the use of Danielic language from the one to the other shows that the two ideas are closely related. The parousia might well be described as the final implementation of Jesus' kingship. But it is not the *beginning* of it, as Matthew has so strikingly indicated in the closing scene of his Gospel where he has the risen Jesus declare while still on earth, in words which echo Daniel 7.14, 'All authority in heaven and on earth has been given to me' (Matt. 28.18). W. D. Davies appropriately interprets Matthew 28.18-20, in the light of its use of Daniel 7 language, as 'the description of the enthronement of the Son of Man', but significantly describes it also as 'a proleptic parousia'.[14] The same might be said of the passages in Mark which we are considering: in using the language of Daniel 7 to speak of his coming enthronement and power Jesus is also laying the foundation for an ultimate demonstration of that kingship in a triumphant return to earth. But that is a later stage, and one which lies beyond the explicit parameters of Daniel 7 and, I would argue, of these Marcan verses as well. The primary reference in all three cases is, I believe, to a situation far more imminent than the parousia or the end of the world.

Mark 8.38; 13.26; 14.62 – Exegesis in Context

Our study of these three key passages based on Daniel 7.13-14 may most conveniently be presented in reverse order.

Mark 14.62

One of the three texts we are considering is quite widely agreed to refer to something more immediate than a parousia at some time in the future. In Mark 14.62 two Old Testament passages are combined in a declaration of the vindication which Jesus expects his judges to be able to see, Psalm 110.1 and Daniel 7.13. Psalm 110.1 is used frequently in the New Testament as a scriptural foundation for the belief of the early Christians that the risen and ascended Jesus is now already installed in the position of supreme power at the right hand of God,[15] and there seems no reason to doubt that the same reference is intended here. Jesus, the prisoner at the bar, facing the enthroned judges of Israel, will soon be seen as the Son of Man himself enthroned in power; then they will have to acknowledge that the tables have been turned, and that the one they condemn will himself be installed as judge, and that by God's own decree.

By including the phrase 'from now on', Matthew and Luke have both made it clear that they do not understand these words of a distant event.[16] But traditional Christian interpretation has thought otherwise, since Jesus goes on to speak of 'coming with the clouds of heaven', and that, as we have seen, has been assumed to be parousia language. True, there has been some embarrassment over just how one can be both 'sitting' and 'coming' at the same time (unless a mobile throne is envisaged!), and it has been more normal to understand the 'coming' as a separate event subsequent to the 'sitting', even though the text does not say so. But once the 'coming' is understood against its background in Daniel 7.13, not as a journey to earth but as an allusion to the enthronement of the Son of Man, the problem disappears, and the two Old Testament texts are found to be talking about the same thing, the sovereignty of the risen and ascended Jesus. That is something which will indeed be true 'from now on', and which Jesus' Sanhedrin judges will soon be in a position to 'see'. New Testament exegesis has increasingly recognized this perspective, and there has been 'a considerable shift of opinion' towards the interpretation of Mark 14.62 as an enthronement text, not a parousia prediction.[17]

Mark 13.26

But if it is likely that the use of the imagery of Daniel 7.13 in Mark
14.62 refers to enthronement rather than parousia, is it not worth
considering whether the prediction of the 'coming of the Son of
Man' which forms the climax of the preceding chapter should be
interpreted in the same light?[18] More than twenty years ago I
proposed an exegesis of the imagery of Mark 13.24-7 along this
line,[19] and I have not yet seen reason to change my view except in
details.[20] Indeed the subsequent development of 'discourse analysis'
approaches to the biblical text has tended to confirm my view of the
flow of argument through Mark 13, taken as a deliberately composed
whole.[21]

It is surely important to recognize that the question from the
disciples (v. 4) to which Jesus' discourse is a reply is concerned
(explicitly at least) with only one subject, the destruction of the
temple which Jesus has just predicted in verse 2.[22] It is therefore
improbable that a new subject (the parousia) will be introduced into
the reply before the first question has been answered, without a
change of subject being clearly marked. And any change of subject is
made even more unlikely by the fact that there is a strongly marked
flow of time-related clauses through the whole discourse up to verse
31. Much of the argument is negative, warning against premature
expectation of the fulfilment of Jesus' prediction ('beware', 'do not
be led astray', it is 'not yet', etc.),[23] but verse 14 seems to introduce
the beginning of the time of fulfilment ('But when you see . . .'), and
it is generally agreed that the reference here and in the following
verses is to the events of the Roman war which began in AD 66.
From there to verse 27 there is no break in the sequence. 'Those
days' (of the siege) in verse 19 prepares for 'But in those days, after
that tribulation' in verse 24, while verses 26 and 27 follow on
directly with 'and then', 'and then'. Here then is the reply to the
'When?' of the disciples' question – and that question, we must
remember, was about the destruction of the temple. The following
verses (vv. 28-31) reflect on the close time-links involved, by means
of the parable of the fig tree (showing that the climax follows
inevitably and quickly once fulfilment has begun) and the clear
declaration that 'all these things' (the phrase the disciples had used

with reference to the destruction of the temple in v. 4) will occur within the generation (v. 30).

In verse 32, however, the wording *does* suggest a change of subject, with a reference to 'that day and hour', when no (singular) day or hour has been referred to in the chapter so far. Admittedly there is still no explicit reference to the parousia (as there is in the parallel in Matthew), but the time being talked about is one of which no one knows, not even Jesus himself. This is in striking contrast to the clearly time-orientated argument of the preceding verses, particularly the explicit limitation to the present generation in verse 30, and suggests that a new theme has been introduced, one which allows no prior warning of the sort Jesus has been giving in the first part of his reply with regard to the destruction of the temple.

It is within such an understanding of the flow of the discourse that it seems worthwhile to consider whether the words of verses 24–7 point as inevitably to the parousia as most commentators have assumed. I cannot here go into detail,[24] but it is my contention that when these words are read in the light of their Old Testament background (and there is scarcely a word of vv. 24–7 which is not clearly drawn from Old Testament prophetic passages) they are most appropriately understood not of the parousia but as a theological interpretation (using standard prophetic and apocalyptic symbolism) of the events of AD 70. The destruction of the capital and temple of the nation which had hitherto been the focus of divine government on earth marked a change in the divine economy so profound as to justify the vivid apocalyptic symbolism of cosmic collapse, which the Old Testament prophets had used of the downfall of Babylon and of other pagan powers. And in this context, by a heavy irony, the enthronement of the one 'like a son of man' (who in Daniel's vision symbolized Israel as the triumphant people of God) denotes the exaltation of Jesus, the true 'Israel', to the place of supreme power, 'coming' to God to receive the universal dominion which was his due. All this would, and did, occur before that generation had passed away.

I realize that so brief a presentation of what must inevitably be a complex and controversial thesis is not likely to carry immediate conviction. But I hope I have given enough of the taste of my perspective on Mark 13 to explain why I cannot accept that a parousia reference is any more essential to the Danielic language of 13.26 than it is to that of 14.62. Both passages, I believe, predict the imminent enthronement of the Son of Man, not his return to earth. Of course his sovereignty will ultimately find its consummation in the parousia, but that is not the focus of the discourse up to verse 31, and is not the subject of the declaration that 'all these things' will occur within that generation. 'The coming of the Son of Man' to the throne of power is much more imminent than his return to earth.

Mark 8.38

The remaining Daniel 7 text in Mark can be dealt with more briefly. If we have been right so far to deny that a reference to 'coming' in such a context must refer to the parousia, there is nothing in the wording of 8.38 itself to indicate whether Jesus is speaking of any specific period or event. The focus is not on a particular time, but on the contrast between 'this adulterous and sinful generation' and the Son of Man installed as king in the presence of his Father and the angels. The aim is to challenge his hearers to a present choice of allegiance, not to prepare them for a future sequence of events.

But if Mark 8.38 in itself is not clearly framed in relation to a particular manifestation of the authority of the Son of Man, its association with the following saying in 9.1 brings it firmly into the time-scale of the generation then living. Unless there is a complete *non sequitur* here (as the traditional chapter break implies!), the 'coming' of the Son of Man into his kingly authority is closely associated with 'the kingship of God having come with power'. What 'some of those standing here' will see is the fulfilment of Daniel 7.13-14, the vindication of the Son of Man whom the leaders of Israel have rejected and killed (8.31) and his investiture with the eternal sovereignty which was rightly his. It is for this reason, no doubt, that Matthew's version of these verses includes the phrase 'the Son of Man coming in his kingship' rather than 'the kingship of God having come with power'. The kingship of God and the kingship of the Son of Man are ultimately the same, for it is as the Son of Man comes to God to receive his kingship that God's own purpose is fulfilled, and his kingship effectively established over 'all peoples, nations, and languages' (Dan. 7.14). This was the great hope of

Israel, and in the enthronement of Jesus, the Son of Man, it is about to be fulfilled. 'This generation will not pass away until all these things have happened' (Mark 13.30).

Fulfilment Now – And Not Yet

Our study of the Daniel 7 passages in Mark, with their focus on a visible fulfilment in the near future, suggests then that perhaps Mark would not have been as surprised as some of his commentators that the parousia did not occur during the first century AD. That was not what he was talking about! Jesus' hearers did see, and indeed so did Mark himself, the Son of Man 'coming' to his kingship and exercising his rule powerfully in the world. That was what Daniel's vision was about, and it was in that sense that Jesus referred to it. Later generations have understood him to have been speaking of a visible descent to earth, but perhaps Mark knew his Old Testament too well to imagine that this was what Daniel, or Jesus, intended.

This does not mean, however, that the parousia hope disappears from the text of the Gospels. Indeed, while I do not think that any of Mark's allusions to Daniel 7 are talking in the first place about the parousia, Matthew does offer us two allusions to Daniel 7 which seem to point that way. In Matthew 19.28 the enthronement of the Son of Man in glory is placed 'in the *palingenesia*', a term which is open to various interpretations, but which seems in some way to look beyond the present earthly scene.[25] And in Matthew 25.31ff. the Son of Man is pictured coming in glory and sitting on the throne as king while all the nations are gathered for judgement and men's final destiny is assigned on the basis of the way they have responded to him. Matthew, then, does seem to understand Daniel 7 as pointing to a fulfilment not merely in the immediate vindication of the Son of Man, but also in the final judgement.

And yet it is Matthew who also offers the most immediate prospect of fulfilment of Daniel's vision, in the allusion to Daniel 7.14 in 28.18, where the risen Jesus is pictured, even before the ascension, as having already received the kingship destined for the Son of Man.

For Matthew, more clearly than for Mark, the 'fulfilment' of Daniel 7.13–14 is not confined to a single event or time, but continues progressively from the time of Jesus' earthly ministry right through to the end of the age, with the kingship of the Son of Man variously manifested throughout the period in the ongoing triumph of the purpose of God. We have considered earlier in this chapter the principle of the 'multiple fulfilment' of biblical prophecy, and here is a clear case of it.

The three allusions to Daniel 7 in Mark all carry with them, as we have seen, more or less explicit time-limitations, and focus on what will be visible within the current generation. But this does not rule out the possibility that Mark, like Matthew, would have recognized that there may be a further dimension to the kingship of the Son of Man beyond that generation. While none of the three passages, as I understand them, speaks primarily about the parousia, it is quite possible that Mark was aware that a more ultimate fulfilment was still to come. It may be for this reason that Mark 13, having focused on the manifestation of Jesus' sovereignty within the generation, goes on to speak (unnecessarily, as it would seem from the disciples' original question) of a day and hour which no one knows, and for which his readers must always be on the alert.

Once this possibility of the multiple fulfilment of prophecy is accepted, the whole scenario of a mistaken Jesus and a disappointed Church from which we began this chapter loses its force. Albert Schweitzer's portrayal of Jesus as the disillusioned prophet of an imminent apocalyptic fulfilment was focused especially on Matthew 10.23, 'you will not have completed all the towns of Israel before the Son of Man comes'. But it is that same Matthew who records Jesus' declaration of the enthronement of the Son of Man in 28.18 (long before they could have 'completed all the towns of Israel'), and it is that enthronement to which the Danielic language of 'coming' primarily points. When eventually he 'comes' at the end of the age, that will be only the final act of a drama of the fulfilment of Daniel 7 which had already begun when the risen Jesus appeared before his followers in the hills of Galilee, and which would be progressively demonstrated as his sovereignty was extended 'in power' during the momentous decades which followed.

The Coming of the Kingdom of God

This long discussion of the 'coming of the Son of Man' may seem to have strayed a long way from our announced subject, the 'kingship of God' and its 'coming in power' within the generation. But Mark himself has guided us in this direction, by the close link he has made between the 'coming of the Son of Man' in 8.38 and the 'coming of the kingship of God with power' in the next verse. Matthew has underlined the connection by his version of the latter saying, which speaks directly of 'the Son of Man coming in his kingship' (Matt. 16.28). What has emerged from our study is the inseparable link between these two ideas, so long separated in New Testament scholarship (see pp. 17–18). It is the role of the Son of Man in Daniel's vision to establish God's sovereignty over all opposing forces, to make actual the eternal kingship of God. In that sense the enthronement of the Son of Man *is* the coming of the kingdom of God with power. And the passages we have been considering declare in different ways that within the lifetime of Jesus' contemporaries that vision will have been fulfilled.

Another passage in Mark which appears to envisage the imminent coming of the kingdom of God is 14.25. Shortly before his death Jesus declares that he will drink no more wine 'until that day when I drink it new in the kingdom of God'. This, like the saying we have been considering above, is introduced by the solemn 'Amen' formula; it is meant to be noticed.

This was Jesus' last meal. It would be possible, therefore, to understand this saying as indicating just that, that he will not drink again on this earth, and in that case 'in the kingdom of God' might be taken to mean simply 'in heaven'. But that would be an unusual use of the phrase in Mark. Most commentators, noticing the specific mention of 'new' wine, see here a reference to the time of salvation and a new creation, and more specifically to the Jewish hope of the 'messianic banquet'.[26] Jesus, about to go to his sacrificial death (14.22–4), looks forward to the time of salvation which must result from it, and in which he expects again to share in table-fellowship with his disciples (Matthew makes this explicit by including the words 'with you' Matt. 26.29), but in the new dimension of the kingdom of God.[27]

But this does not give us any clearer guidance on *when* the kingdom of God is established, since Jesus will no longer be on earth to drink wine during the whole period which will follow from his ascension until his parousia. He will, of course, be with the disciples briefly after his resurrection, as Mark will remind us a few verses later (14.28; cf. Acts 10.41 for the disciples' eating and drinking with him at that time), and Karl Barth suggests that Mark 14.25 refers to that period, when Jesus was to share the new wine of the kingdom of God with his disciples, even before his ascension to heaven.[28] That interpretation would fit in with the view that the coming of the kingdom of God with power was already in a sense true from the time of Jesus' resurrection. But probably Mark 14.25 is not explicit enough to be tied down to a particular period. Nor need it be restricted to the time of the parousia. The concept of progressive fulfilment which we have been exploring makes it not only difficult but also unnecessary for us to give a particular date to Jesus' expectation of the messianic banquet. What is clear in Mark 14.25, as in the rest of Mark's account, is that Jesus and his disciples are already living in the context of the coming of the kingdom of God.

5

'The Government Upon His Shoulder'

One of the most striking messianic prophecies of the Old Testament (and one which, surprisingly, is not directly taken up in the New Testament)[1] speaks of a child to be born:

> and the government will be upon his shoulder . . .
> Of the increase of his government and of peace
>   there will be no end,
> upon the throne of David, and over his kingdom,
>   to establish it, and to uphold it
> with justice and with righteousness
>   from this time forth and for evermore. (Isa. 9.6–7)

Here, as often in the Old Testament and in subsequent Jewish hope, the expectation of the establishment of divine government takes the more specific form of a messianic king, of the line of David, who will exercise royal authority on God's behalf, a vice-regent of the kingship of God.

When Jesus announced the arrival of God's kingship, and in his own ministry demonstrated its authority over the power of evil, it would be surprising if neither he nor those who followed him understood his role in relation to such prophecies. How far, then, does Mark's Gospel allow us to see Jesus not merely as the herald of divine government, but as himself the messianic king upon whose shoulder the government rests?

In the previous chapter we noted Matthew's willingness (alone among the Gospels) to speak directly of the 'kingdom of the Son of Man' (Matt. 13.41; 16.28; 19.28; 25.31, with 34; cf. 20.21), but we noticed also that while that phrase as such is not used in Mark, he has no hesitation in including sayings which envisage the enthronement of the Son of Man in terms drawn from the vision in Daniel 7.13–14. So the kingship of Jesus, not merely the kingship of God, is on the agenda for Mark as well as for Matthew.

'The Coming Kingdom of our Father David'

Isaiah's prophecy of the coming king stated explicitly that his government would be exercised 'upon the throne of David, and over his kingdom', and we have seen in Chapter One that popular expectation of the establishment of the kingship of God was couched largely in nationalistic terms. Such hopes naturally focused on the restoration of the Davidic monarchy and the return of the political supremacy which Israel enjoyed uniquely during the reigns of David and of Solomon, the son of David. When Jesus staged his dramatic entry into Jerusalem, it was this popular hope which came to the surface:

> Those who went ahead and those who followed were crying out:
> 'Hosanna!
> Blessed is he who comes in the name of the Lord!
> Blessed is the coming kingdom of our father David!
> Hosanna in the highest!' (Mark 11.9–10)

This is, in Mark's narrative, the first and only visit which Jesus makes to the capital city of the people of God, and to its temple, the centre of the worship of Israel. He was introduced to us in Mark 1.9 as 'Jesus from Nazareth in Galilee', and his ministry has up to this point been concentrated in and around his home province, even though some people from the south were among the crowds who followed him (3.7–8). Jerusalem has figured in the Gospel only as the source from which the more serious scribal opposition has come (3.22; 7.1), and as the place to which Jesus must at last go to be rejected and killed at the instigation of the leaders of the people of Israel (10.32–4). The journey from the north down to Jerusalem which has occupied chapter 10 has been depicted as a march to humiliation and death. Yet here now is Jesus, the little-known (but already suspect) teacher from the north, escorted into that same city of death with shouts of 'Hosanna!' and the acclamation of the coming kingdom of David.

Mark does not explicitly unravel this paradoxical outcome. But it is possible to read between the lines of his account what is explicit in Matthew, that those who welcomed Jesus with shouts of 'Hosanna!' and those who later shouted for his crucifixion were not the same people. The acclamations, both Mark and Matthew tell us, came from those who were going ahead and following him, that is, from the other Passover pilgrims who were accompanying him into the city, but Matthew 21.10–11 goes on to mention the very different reaction of 'the whole city', which was a puzzled, if not hostile, 'Who is this?', to which 'the crowds' responded by triumphantly introducing *their* leader, 'This is the prophet Jesus, and he is from Nazareth in Galilee.' The provincial rivalry could hardly be more marked: Jesus, the hope of the Galileans, cannot expect a ready welcome in Jerusalem, to which he comes as a stranger. The shouts of his Galilean followers would hardly help to commend him to a city which had a profound suspicion of whatever came from north of Samaria. And the fact that they dared to associate their northern prophet with the kingdom of *David,* the Judaean king, could only make matters worse.[2]

If Mark so understood the situation (and his specification that it was the accompanying crowds who shouted in Jesus' favour suggests that he did), this would explain why he gives no indication of surprise when the Jerusalem crowd later shouts for Jesus' death. What else would you expect in Jerusalem? Similarly, when Jesus is on the cross it is not only the chief priests and the scribes who deride the failed Messiah, but also 'those who went by' in general (15.29–32). All the references to Jerusalem earlier in the Gospel have led us to expect nothing else.

And yet Jesus came willingly to Jerusalem, and presented himself deliberately to the city as its coming king. This was the clear implication of his carefully arranged ride into the city on a donkey, a visual allusion to Zechariah 9.9–10, the prophecy of Jerusalem's victorious prince of peace.[3] It was a bold, dramatic claim to kingship. In Galilee it might have stood more chance of public favour, but it was to Jerusalem that Zechariah's prophecy pictured the king riding, and to Jerusalem Jesus came. He had to do so, because he had not come to lead a Galilean liberation movement, but to restore the kingship of God over his people as a whole. It was to Israel that his mission was directed, and Jerusalem was the centre of the life and worship of Israel. Whatever his place of origin, the messianic king must present himself to his people in the capital.

And the Galileans recognized his meaning, and welcomed his claim. This was 'the coming kingdom of our father David' (11.10). But Jerusalem remained to be convinced.

The Barabbas Factor

One of the most exciting books to emerge from New Testament scholarship in the last few years is Gerd Theissen's 'historical novel', *The Shadow of the Galilean.*[4] It is a resoundingly successful attempt to portray, in fictional form, the context in which Jesus' ministry was set in first-century Palestine. The hero, Andreas, is a Hellenistic Jewish merchant from Sepphoris in Galilee, whose adventures as a reluctant informant for the Roman forces of occupation bring him into contact with many Jewish groups who relate in different ways to the problem of living as the people of God under pagan rule. One of Theissen's most successful ideas is to make Andreas a long-standing friend of Jesus Barabbas, whom he portrays as a high-minded patriot who has committed himself with his eyes open to the course of revolutionary violence against Rome. But Andreas' friendship and respect for Barabbas is tempered by his gradual awareness of another restoration movement, led by one Jesus of Nazareth, who impresses Andreas with his ideology of love for the enemy and his championship of the 'little people'. So Andreas is torn between these two Jesuses, attracted by the other-worldly goodness of the Nazarene, but doubtful whether any improvement to the lot of his people can be achieved without adopting the more activist policy of Barabbas. Thus we see played out in the mind of the fictional Andreas the choice which Pilate posed to the Jerusalem crowd, poignantly expressed in Matthew's version, 'Which [Jesus] do you want me to release to you, Jesus Barabbas or Jesus the so-called Messiah?' (Matt. 27.17).[5]

Barabbas has suffered in Christian tradition from being set up as the foil to Jesus the Messiah. He is generally regarded as a ruffian and a common criminal. But the two men who were crucified with Jesus, and whom tradition reasonably assumes to have been Barabbas' confederates, are described by Mark as *lestai* (Mark 15.27), while John describes Barabbas himself by this same term (John 18.40); *lestes* is certainly a term of reproach, but it is the term which Josephus regularly uses for the Jewish 'freedom fighters' or Zealots (whose ideology he strongly rejected). Moreover, Mark 15.7 mentions that Barabbas' imprisonment was the result of his activities 'in the insurrection'; there is no other record of this particular uprising, but Mark is apparently presenting Barabbas as a leader in a militant patriotic movement. Perhaps Theissen has reacted too strongly against the popular image by making Barabbas such an attractively well-motivated patriot, but his reconstruction of the scene does highlight the differing patterns of divine government with which the people of Jerusalem found themselves confronted.

On the one hand there was the straightforward activism of Barabbas and the Zealots, the philosophy of Judas of Galilee, which saw violence and death as a necessary price to pay for removing the scandal of pagan domination from God's people; and on the other hand the apparently impractical policy of Jesus of Nazareth, the gentle dreamer who called on all men to love one another, and was prepared to die himself, but not to kill, in order to achieve his aim. Of course there was much more to the message of Jesus than that, but perhaps Theissen is not too far from the mark in suggesting that it was in some such terms that an interested outsider might have perceived the alternative programmes for the restoration of Israel.

So when Jesus rode into Jerusalem on the donkey he was not only confronting the likely scepticism of Jerusalem towards a self-proclaimed 'king' who came from Galilee, but he was also inviting comparison with other, more activist, programmes for the restoration of divine government, and his choice of Zechariah 9.9–10 as his 'manifesto' made it plain that his kingship was not of the militant type, but was committed to the establishment of peace among the nations. The people of Jerusalem were faced with a choice which probably most of them did not find very difficult to make. Unlike the Galileans, who had had some opportunity of absorbing the radical implications of Jesus' teaching, they would quickly write Jesus off as a hopeless idealist, whose other-worldly policy had no earthly hope of unseating the might of Rome. And that, for most ordinary Jews, was what the kingship of God was all about.

'Are You the King of the Jews?'

The issue of kingship lay at the heart of both phases of Jesus' trial. In the Jewish trial the issue was inevitably that of Jesus' supposed messianic claim, made clearly but non-verbally in the entry to Jerusalem, reinforced by his high-handed action in the temple (11.15–18), and strongly implied by the parable of the tenants in the vineyard (which the Jewish leaders rightly interpreted as an attack on their own position, 12.12). The issue of authority (11.27–33) was clearly raised by Jesus' cavalier attitude to the institutions and leadership of the Jerusalem establishment, but he had so far avoided an explicit public declaration of who he claimed to be. So the Jewish trial focused on his claims. His supposed threat to the temple (14.57–8) was not only an assault on national values and pride,[6] and a challenge to the existing leadership, but implied also the assumption of the role of the Messiah as restorer of the temple and its worship.[7] So it was no *non sequitur* when the high priest, in the light of the failure to make this charge stick, went on to a direct challenge, 'Are you the Messiah?' (14.61). Jesus' dramatic 'I am' (14.62) marked his abandonment at last of the 'messianic secret'.[8] In the light of his earlier ride into the city it was the only response he could have offered – it was precisely that claim which he had come to Jerusalem to make.

But his reply did not end there, but went on to claim a royal power on a level altogether above that of a Son of David on the throne of Jerusalem, that of the Son of Man sitting at the right hand of Power and coming with the clouds of heaven. We have discussed in the previous chapter the implications of this enthronement language drawn from Psalm 110.1 and Daniel 7.13–14 (pp. 76–7). It picks up the argument of Mark 12.35–7 that the wording of Psalm 110.1

indicates a status for the Messiah far above that of a mere Son of David. The throne of Jesus is not in Jerusalem, but in heaven.

This is kingship language, however, and quite sufficient for the high priest's purposes. Jesus can now be charged before the Roman prefect with claiming to be a king, 'the King of the Jews'. And surely that was just the role in which Jesus *had* presented himself when he rode into the Jewish capital on a donkey. To deny it would be to retract the very claim he had come to Jerusalem to make. He does not retract it, but affirms it, in response to Pilate's question, in the guarded words *Sy legeis*, 'You say it' (15.2). Those two little words have been given interpretations ranging from the strongly affirmative 'You've said it!' to the sarcastically negative 'That's what *you* say.' But I think it is now generally agreed that David Catchpole was right to describe this formula as affirmative but 'reluctant or circumlocutory in formulation'.[9] It is a way of accepting the words used, but dissociating oneself from the way the speaker is likely to have interpreted them: 'Yes, but I do not mean by those words what you mean.' And that is all that Jesus will say. If the Jewish priests did not understand the nature of Jesus' messianic claims, how is Pilate, the pragmatic Roman officer, to grasp what sort of kingship Jesus is talking about? So Jesus goes silently to the cross, hung up between two militant patriots, with a charge-sheet which reads simply, and sarcastically, 'the King of the Jews' (15.26). There he is mocked not only by the written words of the official Roman charge, but by the chief priests ('Let the Messiah, the King of Israel, come down . . .'), by the ordinary passers-by, and even by his patriotic fellow sufferers (15.25–32). The kingship of the Son of Man is nowhere in sight, and the establishment of divine government has been swallowed up in a morass of distortion and incomprehension. Even Jesus himself shouts aloud that he has been abandoned by God, before he dies with a great cry. So where now is the kingship of God?

And yet even at that moment of darkness there is a gleam of truth. It comes in the simple words of a no doubt simple man, a minor Roman officer: 'Truly, this man was the Son of God' (15.39). What those words meant to his pagan mind we can never know. But for Mark and his readers here is the essential dimension which puts the whole appalling scene into perspective. For the purpose of Jesus'

mission from the beginning had not been the establishment of a
human kingdom (in which he would by now have manifestly failed),
but the kingship *of God*. The theme of the hidden nature of that
kingship which has run through the Gospel has now reached its
astonishing climax, in the apparent defeat of all that Jesus' followers
had continued to hope for, despite all his attempts at re-education.
No human orientation can survive such an onslaught of paradox.
No human programme of restoration could embrace this sort of
bouleversement. But that was how the secret of God's kingship had
to work itself out, and now it is revealed in the words of a humble
centurion. Jesus, the so-called 'King of the Jews', is really 'the Son
of God'.

Kingship – Human and Divine

All this seems a long way from the events of five days before. 'The
coming kingdom of our father David' (11.10) has taken on a very
strange shape. Luke 24.21 captures effectively the note of wistful
disillusionment which must have characterized Jesus' followers as
they witnessed his arrest, trial and death: 'We had hoped that he was
the one to redeem Israel.' Such hopes had been alive and strong
when he rode into Jerusalem among the euphoric shouts of his
Galilean entourage, and even during the first few days in Jerusalem
they may have remained alive while Jesus and the Jewish leadership
engaged in a running battle of words to establish where true authority
lay. Jesus may have won the argument, but the official establishment
had won the war, and Jesus' bid for kingship had been brutally put
down. Most of them could not see what the centurion saw, only a bid
for the kingship of Israel which had failed.

Jesus' closest disciples, of course, should have known better.
Many of the pilgrim crowd may not have been aware of Jesus' own
expectation of how his kingship was to be established, but the
disciples knew because he had told them, repeatedly, that he was
coming to Jerusalem to be rejected and killed. We have seen earlier
how difficult they had found it to take in what he was saying, and no
doubt when he staged his royal entry to the city their old hopes

revived, and they may even have dared to believe that he had taken Peter's advice after all, and changed his mind about his 'defeatist' view of his mission. Now at last he was behaving like a real king, and the liberation of Israel might after all be about to take place. 'We had hoped that he was the one to redeem Israel', and those hopes had not been easily abandoned.

But even after they came to Jerusalem Jesus had continued to keep before them his own paradoxical idea of kingship. When the Jewish leaders challenged his authority, he pointedly linked his mission with that of John the Baptist (11.27–33) – and everyone knew what had happened to John the Baptist. The parable of the tenants in the vineyard reaches its climax not in the successful mission of the owner's son, but in his murder (12.1–12). The woman who poured ointment over Jesus' head was not anointing him for a coronation but for a burial (14.3–9). And at the Last Supper his imminent death was symbolically enacted before the disciples, as the means by which the mission of the Servant of God must be carried out (14.22–4). So Jesus was not caught unawares by his arrest, trial and death, and neither should his disciples have been. Whatever the Galilean pilgrims may have understood his ride into the city to mean, his idea of kingship was one which could accommodate, indeed which focused on, the apparent triumph of his enemies and his own humiliation and death.

It is the dimension of *God's* kingship which makes sense of this paradoxical mission. Human politics can make no sense of it, but it was not a human political revolution that Jesus had come to stage. Again and again through Mark's account of the last week in Jerusalem the note of divine government is sounded, and the values and policies of human government are overturned.

When Jesus' authority is questioned by 'the chief priests, the scribes and the elders' (an impressive listing of all the main authority groups within the subject nation of Israel, who together made up its supreme council, the Sanhedrin), he replies with the simple alternative of authority being given 'from heaven or from men' (11.30). His own authority, he implies, is like that of John the Baptist, 'from heaven', and therefore he needs no endorsement by men, even the men of the Sanhedrin itself. John's heavenly authority had led him into conflict with men, and Jesus can expect no better treatment (cf. 9.12–13). He goes on immediately to direct the parable of the tenants against these same human authorities, who will kill the owner's son, and concludes it with a quotation from Psalm 118.22, which sums up the whole theme of the paradox of divine government which we have found running through so much of the Gospel:

> The very stone which the builders rejected
>   has become the head of the corner;
> this was the Lord's doing,
>   and it is marvellous in our eyes. (Mark 12.10–11)

Here again is the language of reversal, of the overturning of human valuation, of the first who are last and the last first. It was this that the centurion at the cross was able to see against all human expectation. The messenger who has been rejected and killed is, after all, the son of the owner of the vineyard, and it will be the owner who has the final word.

The divine perspective breaks in again when Jesus challenges the normal human understanding of the Messiah as the Son of David (12.35–7). To see the Messiah in that light is to start at the wrong end, to view him as just another human king. But he has been appointed by 'the Lord' himself to a position above that even of David; so how can he be 'David's son'? The pronouncement is frustratingly brief and cryptic. In Matthew's version it includes the question 'Whose son is he?' (Matt. 22.42), and perhaps there is a hint there of the status of the Messiah as Son of God, which has already been raised by the parable of the tenants, and which will come to the surface both in the Sanhedrin trial and in the centurion's declaration at the cross. But this implication is not so easily found in Mark's version. The point is rather that a mere human valuation of the Messiah will miss the most important thing about him, that his role is given him by God.

Another theme which runs strongly through the Jerusalem chapters of Mark's Gospel and which also points away from human to divine government is that of Jesus' relation to the temple. The temple is the first place Jesus visits when he arrives in the city (11.11), and is the site of the public teaching and debates which take up much of chapters 11 – 12 (11.27; 12.35,41; 13.1). As the centre of national life and worship it was the obvious place for him to go. But from the beginning Jesus seems to be embarking on a polemic against the temple. The daring one-man demonstration which he launched against the misuse of the temple (11.15–18) was indeed in its defence, as the 'house of prayer for all nations' which God had designed it to be; but it was so no longer, and it was the temple as it currently operated which was the object of Jesus' attack.[10] By carefully interweaving Jesus' action in the temple with the cursing and destruction of the fig tree,[11] Mark helps his readers to see the latter as a symbolic act of judgement on the temple establishment which holds out great promise, but bears no fruit (cf. the parable of the tenants).[12] Israel as Jesus finds it is bearing 'nothing but leaves', and the temple is the focus of its failure. So when eventually Jesus leaves the temple and sits opposite it on the Mount of Olives,[13] it is to predict its total destruction, and to go on, as I have argued in the previous chapter (pp. 78–80), to describe that destruction in terms of the establishment of the kingship of the Son of Man. The old order of the temple with its earthly hierarchy is finished, and the new order of divine government takes its place.

The charge against Jesus at his trial that he had planned to destroy and to replace the temple is, technically, false (14.57) – as far as our records go he never threatened to destroy it himself. But he did say that it would be destroyed (13.2), and point forward to a new order which was soon to replace it, and Mark delicately indicates this theme even in the context of the false charge by including the words 'made with hands' and 'not made with hands' to characterize the old and new temples (14.58). Here again is the contrast between human and divine institutions.[14] The old temple, even though built at God's command, was never more than a human structure, and was in the end dispensable. But what Jesus is bringing in its place is of a different order altogether, not made with hands. False charge as it was, it enshrined an important truth about the mission of Jesus, and that truth was dramatically demonstrated at the moment of Jesus' death, when the curtain of the temple was torn apart, and the sanctuary made with hands was thrown open (15.38). And, lest we miss the point, Mark informs us that the tear was made 'from top to bottom', as only God could do it. The desecration of the temple by no human hand (to which its destruction by the Romans a generation later was merely a human endorsement) opened the way for a new temple not made with hands. And it was when the Roman centurion saw *this* that he was able to say of the dead Jesus, 'he was the Son of God' (15.39). The divine dimension is, ultimately, the one that counts. Divine government is reaching its fulfilment even in the moment of the death of the Son of God.

In Chapter Three we considered the theme of Jesus' reversal of human values as one of the results of the implementation of divine government. What we have seen in this section is that this 'bouleversement of the value scale' is operative not only in the values which God's kingship instills in those who enter it, but also in the very process by which it is established. It is a crazy, topsy-turvy programme in which rejection is the way to glory and death the way of victory, in which a cross becomes a throne, and a dying Son of Man is recognized by the most unlikely onlooker as the Son of God. It is at the climax of such a paradoxical mission that Jesus can construct with bread and wine an enactment of his imminent death, and at the same time state that when he next drinks wine God's kingship will be already established (14.25).

So whatever exactly Jesus had in mind when he rode on the donkey into Jerusalem, it was something very different from the human establishment of the revolutionary government which was the hope of the Zealots and, no doubt, of many of his Galilean followers. And when Mark recorded the pilgrims' ecstatic welcome of 'the coming kingdom of our father David' (11.10), he at least, even if not they, had in mind a very different sort of kingdom. Jesus was a king indeed, for so he was claiming in all but explicit words, but not that sort of king. He could not deny Pilate's charge that he claimed to be 'the king of the Jews', but his understanding of those words was poles apart from Pilate's: 'So *you* say.'

Mark gives us no indication that the people of Jerusalem understood the nature of Jesus' claim any more than Pilate did. We can hardly blame them for that, when the closest of Jesus' Galilean followers had barely begun to come to terms with it, even after intensive teaching. The 'human thoughts' (8.33) with which Peter had responded to Jesus' first announcement of his paradoxical mission were still very much alive (and, according to Luke, would still be alive even after his death, when the disciples were to ask the risen Jesus, 'Lord, is it time now for you to restore the kingship to Israel?', Acts 1.6). If they found the reorientation so hard, it is no wonder that the Jerusalem crowd, newly introduced to the prophet of Nazareth, had little difficulty in seeing it was not he but Barabbas who was their man.

When Judas Iscariot changed sides in the course of that final week, it seems likely that one of the main reasons was his increasing awareness that Jesus' vision of divine government was not going to conform to his own, that the hopes of the Galilean pilgrims who shouted in Jesus' support on their arrival in Jerusalem were bound to be disappointed, because Jesus had never seen his mission in the way they did. Judas was probably the only non-Galilean among the twelve,[15] and this may have been a factor in his decision to dissociate himself from company which, now they were in Jerusalem, was likely to prove embarrassing. But surely there was more to it than that: Judas had reluctantly come to the conclusion, like Theissen's Barabbas, that for all the attractiveness of Jesus' unwordly ethic, his approach had no realistic hope of changing the way things were in the real world of power politics. To continue to support Jesus could not, therefore, bring in the kingship of God, as Judas understood it; and in that case it would be better for Jesus to be eliminated, and with him the delusive promise that Israel could be restored to its divinely intended role by loving your enemies instead of fighting them.

So the establishment of God's kingship remained a secret, partially grasped only by a minority of those who heard Jesus' words and watched his dramatic ride into Jerusalem. And even that minority proved unable to cope with the way things developed once they were in Jerusalem, as all Jesus' paradoxical predictions, which they had never really come to terms with, proved only too true. 'They all forsook him, and fled' (14.50). At the moment of Jesus' death there seems to have been no one there who could understand the divine secret – except, in his own remarkable way, the Roman centurion!

It is a question worth pondering whether even today the secret of divine government is any more easily grasped, in a world in which the first are still first and the last last, and where human politics leave little room for the exercise of God's kingship.

'His Name will be Called . . . Mighty God'

We began this chapter with Isaiah 9.6–7, the prophecy of a coming king on the throne of David, and we have seen how Mark, while not referring to that prophecy, presents Jesus to us as the one whose role it was to establish God's kingship among his people. The divine government which Jesus announced as he began his ministry in Galilee was in fact destined to rest upon his own shoulder, though in a way which would have made no more sense to those who first heard Isaiah's prophecy than it did to Jesus' own contemporaries.

But Isaiah 9.6–7 is remarkable among the Old Testament prophecies of a Davidic Messiah in that the coming king whom it presents is described in terms too high for any ordinary human king, too high even, one would have thought, for courtly flattery, at least among the worshippers of the one true God. It was one thing for an Egyptian pharaoh to be hailed as a god; after all, one additional god in a large pantheon is no great innovation. But for Jewish monotheism to envisage a man to whom the titles 'Mighty God' and 'Everlasting Father' could be applied is extraordinary, and no other Old Testament passage goes quite so far in this direction. In subsequent Jewish thought, while a variety of 'intermediary' figures were thought of as operating as God's chief agent on earth, and thus as occupying a uniquely exalted position alongside God himself, none of these figures were thought of as being themselves divine, and the proper recipients of worship; that was the jealously guarded prerogative of God alone.[16] Isaiah 9.6–7 is thus pointing towards a new and remarkable extension of the messianic hope, that of a Davidic king who is himself no less than divine.

It was this direction that Christian theology eventually took, in its understanding of the man Jesus as God incarnate. It was a momentous change, which involved redrawing the whole map of Jewish theology to accommodate two persons, and then three, within the limits of monotheism. Much of recent study of New Testament Christology has been devoted to trying to trace the origins of this bold new theology, or, to use Larry Hurtado's biological metaphor, this 'binitarian mutation' within Jewish monotheism.[17] Scholars in the earlier part of this century saw this as a later development under the influence of pagan Hellenistic thought, which introduced an alien concept into the pure monotheism of Jewish Christianity. But Paul's letters, written by a Jewish Christian in the middle years of the first century, have remained a stubborn obstacle to this view, and the more so when some of their most remarkable expressions of a high Christology are recognized not as Paul's own words but as his approving adoption of already existing Christian formulae.[18] Already in the pre-Pauline churches it seems that Jesus was the recipient of prayer and the object of worship, and was spoken of in terms which are appropriate only to God himself.[19] Indeed in recent discussion the point has rightly been emphasized that Christian worship of the risen Jesus was the source rather than the product of the incarnational language of New Testament Christology, that devotion preceded formulation; it was because Christians in the early decades of the growth of the Church were already worshipping and experiencing Jesus as God that they eventually found it necessary to expand their monotheistic theology to accommodate the idea of God incarnate.[20]

It is well known that the direct description of Jesus as 'God' is rare in the New Testament, and is mostly to be found in what are generally thought to be the latest books to be written.[21] Even if this is so (and I do not think the case is as clear-cut as that),[22] I would not find it surprising. It is one thing to be drawn to recognize Jesus as a proper object of worship, but another to put that conviction into the stark form of a statement that 'Jesus is God', when all the inbred instincts of your Jewish faith cry out against such startling language, and when your fellow Jews are bound to find it not only offensive but incomprehensible. But I believe that it is possible to trace the development of a divine estimation of Jesus back to a much earlier period than that of self-conscious 'Jesus-is-God' formulation, and I would like to suggest now that even Mark's Gospel, normally thought to present the least developed Christology of all the Gospels, enables us to see some of the basis on which the full-blown incarnational and ultimately trinitarian language of the early Church was founded.

Mark and the Divinity of Jesus

A Gospel may seem an unlikely place to look for data on the divinity of Jesus. It was, after all, after the resurrection that Christians began to speak of Jesus as 'the Lord', and to worship him as such.[23] But the Gospels record events *before* the resurrection; and this is especially true of Mark, which notoriously lacks any accounts of post-resurrection appearances of Jesus, the one place where 'worship' might seem more likely to occur in the narrative context. It is hardly to be expected that Jesus of Nazareth, walking as a man among men, should be worshipped or referred to as 'God' during the years leading up to his death in Jerusalem. It is true, of course, that the Authorized Version has Jesus 'worshipped' at several points in Matthew's Gospel, but it is now agreed that the verb *proskyneo* need have no divine connotations, but represents the sort of 'courtesy' appropriate to a superior human being. And in any case, Mark does not use the verb of approaches to Jesus by other people (except for the facetious 'homage' of the Roman guards, 15.19) – only of the approach of Legion (5.6), who represents supernatural rather than human insight (cf. 1.24,34; 3.11).

So formal worship of a human being on earth is hardly to be expected, particularly in Mark's Gospel, where there is such emphasis on Jesus' secrecy and on the weakness and hiddenness of the coming of God's kingship through his ministry. But it may none the less be appropriate to look in Mark's story for aspects of Jesus' life and teaching which would provide the impetus for recognizing him later, after his death and resurrection, as more than just an ordinary man. And of course Mark himself is writing in the light of Easter and of all that followed, so that, however inappropriate language of God incarnate might be to the narrative setting, he may tell his story with some Christological hindsight.

It is instructive, for instance, to turn again to the prologue (1.1–13), from which we began (pp. 8–10). I referred then to those opening verses as a glimpse behind the scenes, enabling Mark's readers to understand, in a way that was not open to the participants in the story, who Jesus really is. One aspect of those verses which I hinted at then may be brought more clearly into focus here. The Gospel opens with a quotation attributed to 'Isaiah', though of course only the latter part of the words quoted comes from that prophet. This is the only scriptural quotation in the whole Gospel which Mark offers as his own editorial contribution, rather than as an utterance by Jesus. Its position as the opening statement of the Gospel means that it is meant to be noticed, as a key to understanding the story to follow. And yet it is not, as we might have expected, a quotation about Jesus as Messiah, but about the forerunner, who is immediately identified as John the Baptist. Indeed it apparently leaves no room for the Messiah at all, since the two main texts which make up this composite quotation (Mal. 3.1; Isa. 40.3; the quotation of Mal. 3.1 is woven together with words from Exod. 23.20) speak of someone who prepares the way directly for the coming of God himself.[24] If John the Baptist has fulfilled that role, the next act of the drama ought to be the coming of *God*. It is true that John speaks of a 'stronger one' who comes after him, and who will baptize with Holy Spirit, and with Christian hindsight we understand that the 'stronger one' is Jesus. But John does not say that he is speaking of another man, and in the light of the preceding quotations it would be more natural to understand that the 'stronger one' is the God for whose coming he has prepared the way (and who had promised that in the last days he would pour out his Spirit: Isa. 32.15; 44.3; Ezek. 36.26-7; 39.29; Joel 2.28-9). Thus Mark has led us to expect an account of the coming of God to judge and to save his people, and when the next verse tells us that *'Jesus* came' there are obvious and startling implications for the reader to draw, particularly as the same pericope goes on to record God's identification of Jesus as his 'beloved Son'.

The hints thus offered in the prologue are amply filled out as the story develops. We have mentioned Jesus' authority over demons, and their recognition of him as 'the holy one of God', 'the Son of the most high God' (1.24; 5.7; cf. 3.11). Humans too are obliged to recognize the unique authority both of his healing and his teaching (e.g. 1.22, 27). The issue comes to a head in his claim to forgive sins, which the scribes regard as blasphemous, since 'Who can forgive sins except God alone?'; Jesus does not dispute the theology of their objection, but proves his ability to forgive sins by adding an instant physical healing as well (2.1-12). He goes on to declare himself 'Lord of the sabbath', which God himself had instituted

(2.28). Jesus thus appears to be arrogating to himself nothing less than divine authority. A similar implication attaches to his claim that 'Heaven and earth will disappear, but my words will not disappear' (13.31), since it was precisely this unending authority which the Old Testament prophets attributed to the word of God, in distinction from all human utterances (Isa. 40.8).

To discern a note of divine authority in the claim that 'the Son of Man is Lord of the sabbath' may seem rather quixotic, since the essential meaning of the phrase 'a son of man' is a human being, indeed a human being in explicit contrast with divinity. The phrase is so used throughout the book of Ezekiel to distinguish the prophet, as 'mere man', from the God on whose behalf he speaks. Some have argued that it is this sense of mortal frailty, rather than any claim to authority, which is essential to the understanding of Jesus' choice of the title 'the Son of Man' for himself.[25] It will have become clear in the previous chapter, however, that I continue to believe that the primary background for Jesus' use of the title is the vision of Daniel 7.13–14, where the 'human being' is so described in contrast not so much to God as to the four beasts whose kingship he supersedes. In this vision, paradoxically perhaps but certainly intentionally, the most important truth about the 'one like a son of man' is not human frailty, but rather a divinely given authority and eternal kingship. He is, as Jewish interpreters around the time of Jesus unanimously recognized, a figure of majesty and triumph.[26] Some recent interpretation of this figure goes further, and insists that, whatever the dictionary meaning of 'a son of man', Daniel's vision is of one who is super-human. This tendency is summed up in the title of Seyoon Kim's important monograph, *The "Son of Man" as the Son of God*, and is more fully worked out in Chrys Caragounis' boldly untraditional study of *The Son of Man*, in which he concludes that Daniel's 'one like a son of man' is 'a heavenly Being with honours and powers normally predicated of God'.[27]

It would, of course, be wrong to suppose that Jesus' interpretation and use of any Old Testament figure must be confined within the parameters of the original author's vision, but the clearly deep influence of the vision of Daniel 7 in Jesus' understanding of his mission as the Gospels portray it suggests that his use of the title 'the Son of Man' should be interpreted primarily against the background of heavenly glory and divine authority. And in fact, as we saw in the previous chapter, in those passages in Mark where the influence of Daniel 7 is most apparent it is the coming enthronement and glory of the Son of Man which is in view. It is that fact, of course, which gives such a striking note of paradox to Jesus' predictions that *the Son of Man* must be rejected and killed. The path of heavenly glory will not take the form that most readers of Daniel would have supposed. But the use of this title at all lifts Jesus' mission from the level of mere human conquest to that of the heavenly figure whose proper role it is to share the throne of God himself. If the 'Son of Man' language in Mark's Gospel is understood against its Old Testament background, it takes its place as part of Mark's presentation of Jesus as more than human.

The main vehicle of this theology in Mark, however, is signalled in his very first verse: 'The beginning of the good news of Jesus Christ, *the Son of God*.'[28] This title, thus declared at the very beginning and endorsed by the voice from heaven in 1.11, recurs at important points throughout the Gospel until it emerges remarkably, as we have seen above (pp. 91–2) in the confession of the centurion at the cross (15.39). Here is the real truth about Jesus, which those around him have been slow to perceive, but which Mark's readers, with their privileged insight through the prologue, should be able to see increasingly confirmed as the story proceeds. It has been obvious to the demons, with their supernatural perception of the true nature of their adversary (3.11; 5.7; cf. 1.24). It has been implied in some of Jesus' public statements, about the son of the owner of the vineyard (12.1–12), and about the status of the Messiah as more than a son of David (12.35–7). It has been explicit in the challenge of the high priest at Jesus' trial, to which Jesus has given a clearly affirmative reply, even though preferring to retain the title 'the Son of Man' (14.61–2). But above all it has twice been declared by God himself (1.11; 9.7) – and you can hardly have a more authoritative witness than that!

Those who are familiar with the gospel stories are liable to miss the quite exceptional nature of those two occasions. While in many of the incidents Mark records there are supernatural or miraculous elements, the scene in which they are set remains firmly earthly and everyday. But on these two occasions heaven invades the earth, at least in the form of vision. At Jesus' baptism he sees heaven torn open, and both visual and auditory contact is made with earth, in the visible descent of the Spirit and the voice from heaven. At the transfiguration Jesus is seen in unearthly splendour, in company with exalted patriarchs from Old Testament days, and again the voice of God comes out of the cloud, the Old Testament symbol of divine presence. These are not just two episodes in the story of Jesus. They are, for those privileged to witness them, moments of revelation, introductions to the world of supernatural reality. In each case the climax of the revelation comes in an audible utterance of God himself (something which occurs nowhere else in the Gospel). And in each case the subject of that utterance is the identity and status of Jesus, as *the Son of God*. Here, if anywhere, we have the ultimate truth about Jesus.

Scholars have long pointed out that human beings could be called 'sons of God' in many ancient cultures, including that of the Jews. The king was occasionally so called in the Old Testament (2 Sam. 7.14; Ps. 2.7) and so was the nation of Israel as a whole (Exod. 4.22; Hos. 11.1). There was even the beginning in post-biblical wisdom writings of the idea that a righteous individual could be described as a son of God (Ben Sira 4.10; Wisdom 2.18).[29] But what we see in Mark is not such a tentative use of honorific language, but the declaration of the unique status of a specific individual by those in a position to know, and above all, twice over, his formal designation as 'my Son' by God himself. Mark's centurion may not, in historical reality, have had any such theological insight, but in this climactic position in Mark's account of the gradual revelation of the secret of Jesus' identity, there can be no doubt that he expected his readers to see in these words an affirmation of what God had already twice declared with his own voice. To be 'Son of God' in this context is to be more than human.

The sequel confirms it. Mark gives little explicit hint of the theology of the resurrection, though he has carefully included the rising after three days as the regular climax to the predictions of Jesus' suffering and death (8.31; 9.31; 10.34), so that when the event is recorded in chapter 16 the reader can see it as the proper culmination of Jesus' mission, and the confirmation that his suffering and death have been undertaken in obedience to the will of God. But the resurrection also marks the point when the truth about Jesus which was privately disclosed to the disciples on the mountain may be more widely proclaimed (9.9). The vision of his glory, and his designation as the Son of God, which had hitherto been kept secret, could now be openly declared, because the event had proved them true.

The Kingdom of God and the Kingship of Jesus

Our discussion of Mark's view of the identity of Jesus may seem to have taken us a long way from our subject of the kingdom of God. But in fact it has now brought us back to the subject. For we have seen that the man who proclaimed the arrival of God's kingship in Mark 1.15 is presented in the story that follows as himself a king. His kingship is misunderstood and rejected by those around him, and finally finds its unthinkable culmination in his execution as a rebel against Rome, the very concept of kingship from which he had so clearly distanced himself. But beyond that apparent anticlimax he has pointed to another level of kingship altogether, and one to which his earthly humiliation will mysteriously prove the appointed means, the heavenly enthronement of the Son of Man. And his kingship *is* the kingship of God, for it is the Ancient of Days who will place him on the throne. Not only does the Son of Man come as the one who opens the way for God to be known as king; he is himself the agent of that kingship. The government is upon his shoulder. As God's Son, he occupies by right his Father's throne, for he is himself no less than God.

All this was there, in embryo, when Jesus the Galilean began to preach about the coming of divine government. To most of those who heard him the secret of God's kingship remained hidden, but the seed began to grow, by its own power. Now, a generation later, Mark, who is one of those to whom the secret of God's kingship has been given, can already see that the kingdom of God has come with power; the mustard seed is already a fine shrub, and it is still growing. And so he calls his readers to share in the good news of Jesus Christ, the Son of God, and so to enter into God's kingship.

And they have done so, in increasing numbers, so that the revolutionary values of divine government have been brought to bear on the kingdoms of this world. But still the seed must grow, until all people acknowledge Jesus as the Son of God, the ruler at his Father's right hand. Then, at last, at a day and an hour which no one yet knows except God himself, the world will see in the parousia of the Son of Man the ultimate fulfilment of Daniel's great vision, when 'all peoples, nations, and languages . . . [will] serve him', for

> his dominion is an everlasting dominion,
> which shall not pass away,
> and his kingdom one
> that shall not be destroyed. (Dan. 7.14)

Notes

The following abbreviations are used in the Notes: *BJRL Bulletin of the John Rylands University Library of Manchester; EQ Evangelical Quarterly; ExpT Expository Times; JBL Journal of Biblical Literature; JSNT Journal for the Study of the New Testament; JTS Journal of Theological Studies; NTS New Testament Studies; TDNT* G. Kittel and G. Friedrich (eds), *Theological Dictionary of the New Testament* and *ZNW Zeitschrift für die neutestamentliche Wissenschaft.*

Introduction

1. See below, pp. 11–14, for reasons for describing 'the kingdom of God' as a misleading translation of *he basileia tou theou.*
2. This was the title of books by N. Perrin and by G. Lundström, both published in 1963 (by SCM Press and Oliver & Boyd respectively). For some subsequent examples, see also G. E. Ladd, *Jesus and the Kingdom* (London: Harper, 1964); N. Perrin, *Jesus and the Language of the Kingdom* (Philadelphia: Fortress Press/ London: SCM Press, 1976); G. R. Beasley-Murray, *Jesus and the Kingdom of God* (Grand Rapids: Wm B. Eerdmans/Exeter: Paternoster Press, 1986). None of these books offers a separate discussion of each of the three Synoptic Gospels.
3. The most comprehensive recent attempt to study the kingdom of God in Mark is A. M. Ambrozic, *The Hidden Kingdom: A Redaction-Critical Study of the References to the Kingdom of God in Mark's Gospel* (Washington DC: Catholic Biblical Association of America, 1972); cf. also W. H. Kelber, *The Kingdom in Mark: A New Place and a New Time* (Philadelphia: Fortress Press, 1974).
4. I have set out my approach to the Synoptic Problem briefly in my *The Gospel According to Matthew*, Tyndale New Testament

Commentary (Leicester: Inter-Varsity Press/Grand Rapids: Wm B. Eerdmans, 1985), pp. 34–8, and more fully in my *Matthew: Evangelist and Teacher* (Exeter: Paternoster Press, 1989), pp. 24–49. It owes most to the work of J. A. T. Robinson, *Redating the New Testament* (London: SCM Press, 1976), pp. 93–117.

5. A significant pointer to this new trend was D. M. Rhoads and D. M. Michie, *Mark as Story: An Introduction to the Narrative of a Gospel* (Philadelphia: Fortress Press, 1982). This approach was helpfully integrated with more traditional methods of study by E. Best, *Mark: The Gospel as Story* (Edinburgh: T. & T. Clark, 1983). Several more recent works have followed the direction indicated by the titles of these two books.

1 God Rules!

1. Probably the majority of recent interpreters regard Mark 1.1–13 as the 'prologue'. R. H. Lightfoot's influential espousal of this view (on grounds of content rather than formal characteristics) has been reinforced particularly by the observation that this section is held together by the recurrence of two key words, 'Spirit' and 'wilderness', the former of which appears very seldom in the rest of the Gospel and the latter not at all. These verses therefore present a (symbolically powerful) location distinct from that of the narrative which follows, and focus on the supernatural dimension which will underlie the succeeding ministry. An alternative view of the prologue as extending to verse 15 is offered, e.g., by H. Anderson, *The Gospel of Mark* (London: Marshall, Morgan & Scott, 1976), pp. 63–4 and by R. A. Guelich, *Mark 1–8:26,* Word Biblical Commentary (Dallas: Word, 1989), pp. 4–5.

2. According to Josephus, no less than four of the high priests of the first century AD were called Jesus. A rough count of the personal names of characters appearing in Josephus' *Life* (after allowing for uncertainty as to whether certain references are to the same or a different person) produces the following list of the most common names among Josephus' associates (second half of first century AD): Jesus, 4–6; Simon, 3–5; Levi, 4; Jonathan, 3; Herod, 3.

3. The passages usually seen as alluded to in these words are Isaiah 42.1 and Psalm 2.7. These would involve the concepts of the Servant of Yahweh and of the messianic king as Son of God. A further possible allusion to Genesis 22.2 would introduce the theme (important in post-biblical Jewish theology) of the offering of Isaac.

4. The symbolic and psychological importance of the 'wilderness' theme is explored especially by U. Mauser, *Christ in the Wilderness* (London: SCM Press, 1963). Not only John's movement but several other movements of national renewal (and of political revolt against Rome) began in the Jordan 'wilderness' according to Josephus (cf. Acts 21.37–8).

5. For the negative connotation of wild animals over against angels, cf. Psalm 91.12–13; Testament of Naphthali, 8.4. If the latter text is part of the Christian colouring of the Testaments, it would represent an early Christian exegesis of Mark 1.13.

6. These are the titles of a recent series of books on 'the essentials of Christian discipleship' by John Wimber, published by Hodder and Stoughton.

7. The Oxford English Dictionary gives the first meaning of 'kingdom' as 'Kingly function, authority or power; sovereignty, kingship', but correctly describes the usage as 'obsolete' (last attested in 1679!). As in many instances, the subsequent development of usage has left the familiar AV wording behind, so that what was once a good translation is now misleading. It is unfortunate that the standard modern translations have failed to notice the shift of meaning.

8. *God in Strength* (Freistadt: F. Plöchl, 1977; repr. Sheffield: JSOT Press, 1987) is the title of Chilton's study of 'Jesus' Announcement of the Kingdom' (*sic*!), which draws heavily on the background to such language in the targum tradition. The phrases quoted are on pp. 89, 283 of that book, and p. 5 of B. D. Chilton and J. I. H. McDonald, *Jesus and the Ethics of the Kingdom* (London: SPCK, 1987).

9. G. R. Beasley-Murray, *Jesus and the Kingdom of God* (Grand Rapids: Wm B. Eerdmans, 1986).

10. ibid., 339.

11. There are of course references to other 'kingdoms', that of Herod Antipas in 6.23, that of David in 11.10, and, by implication, that of Satan in 3.24, while human kingdoms in general are mentioned in 13.8. (There is also a further mention of 'the kingdom of God' in some manuscripts of 1.14, where 'the gospel of God' is expanded to 'the gospel of the kingdom of God' (or even, in a handful of late manuscripts 'the gospel of the kingdom'!). This reading is generally agreed to be a scribal adaptation of the unusual phrase 'the gospel of God' to parallel the more familiar language of such texts as Matt. 4.23; 9.35.)

12. For a useful discussion of how sayings about 'entering the kingdom of God' are to be understood in relation to a 'dynamic' view of the kingdom of God as God's 'kingly power', see J. Marcus, 'Entering into the Kingly Power of God', *JBL* 107 (1988), pp. 663–75.

13. N. Perrin, *Jesus and the Language of the Kingdom* (Philadelphia: Fortress Press, 1976), pp. 16–32. Perrin's use of the language of 'symbol' has been criticized, e.g. by D. C. Allison, *The End of the Ages Has Come* (Philadelphia: Fortress Press, 1985), pp. 107–12, on the grounds that it does not do justice to the expectation of a definite future event which is essential to some of the synoptic sayings about the kingdom of God. While this may be a fair criticism of Perrin's overall argument, his account of the evocative power of 'kingdom of God' as a symbol is not at all incompatible with a well-defined hope for that kingship to be decisively implemented in the future.

14. Beasley-Murray, *Jesus and the Kingdom of God*, pp. 3–62.

15. D. C. T. Sheriffs, '"A Tale of Two Cities" – Nationalism in Zion and Babylon', *Tyndale Bulletin* 39 (1988), p. 41 (part of a study of 'national ideology in Zion and Babylon' – Sheriffs rightly understands the kingdom of God in Daniel in strongly nationalistic terms).

16. See especially the study by C. C. Caragounis, *The Son of Man: Vision and Interpretation* (Tübingen: Mohr, 1986), pp. 237–8.

17. Beasley-Murray, *Jesus and the Kingdom of God*, chapters 4 and 13.

18. Caragounis, *The Son of Man*, p. 243, summarizing the argument especially of pp. 232–42.

19. See J. Riches, *Jesus and the Transformation of Judaism* (London: Darton, Longman & Todd, 1980), pp. 95–6.

20. See J. Jeremias, *New Testament Theology I: The Proclamation of Jesus* (ET, London: SCM Press, 1971), pp. 198–9. A few other Jewish texts which use 'kingdom of God' language of a future event are cited by Allison, *The End of the Ages has Come*, p. 103.

21. See S. C. Neill and N. T. Wright, *The Interpretation of the New Testament, 1861–1986* (Oxford University Press, 1988), pp. 379–403, for an account by Tom Wright of what he has called the 'Third Quest of the Historical Jesus'. Wright focuses on the work of Ben Meyer (*The Aims of Jesus*), Anthony Harvey (*Jesus and the Constraints of History*), Marcus Borg (*Conflict, Holiness and Politics in the Teachings of Jesus*) and E. P. Sanders (*Jesus and Judaism*). Other names which might appropriately be added to the list of those who have helped to redirect New Testament

scholarship in the direction of taking Jesus' Jewish environment more seriously include Geza Vermes (*Jesus the Jew*), John Riches (*Jesus and the Transformation of Judaism*), and James Charlesworth (*Jesus Within Judaism*), while Gerd Theissen's *The Shadow of the Galilean* (ET, London: SCM Press, 1987) has vividly brought to life for a non-specialist readership Jesus' setting in first-century Palestine.

22. B. F. Meyer, *The Aims of Jesus* (London: SCM Press, 1979), pp. 133–4.

23. Quoted by Riches, *Jesus and the Transformation of Judaism*, p. 97.

24. Josephus, *Jewish War*, II, 118; cf. *Antiquities*, XVIII, 4–10, 23.

25. Riches, *Jesus and the Transformation of Judaism*, p. 100.

26. D. Wenham, *The Parables of Jesus* (London: Hodder & Stoughton, 1989), pp. 20–5. The 'revolution' terminology is exploited throughout the book.

27. For this usage, see G. Dalman, *The Words of Jesus* (ET, Edinburgh: T. & T. Clark, 1902), pp. 100–1; Jeremias, *New Testament Theology I*, p. 102; Chilton, *God in Strength*, pp. 86–9.

28. Meyer, *The Aims of Jesus*, pp. 136–7.

29. Jeremias, *New Testament Theology I*, p. 102.

30. W. F. Albright and C. S. Mann, *Matthew*, Anchor Bible (New York: Doubleday, 1971), pp. 24–5; C. S. Mann, *Mark*, Anchor Bible (New York: Doubleday, 1986), p. 206. See however some cautionary comments on the interpretation of *engizo* by C. C. Caragounis, 'Kingdom of God, Son of Man and Jesus' Self-Understanding', *Tyndale Bulletin* 40 (1989), pp. 12–15.

31. For a useful discussion of the debate on this point in scholarship up to 1970, see A. M. Ambrozic, *The Hidden Kingdom: A Redaction-Critical Study of the References to the Kingdom of God in Mark's Gospel* (Washington DC: Catholic Biblical Association of America, 1972), pp. 15–23. Ambrozic concludes in favour of 'has come'.

32. cf. Allison, *The End of the Ages Has Come*, pp. 104–6, for a useful reminder that already in Jewish thought it was possible to see the eschatological consummation as taking place over an extended time.

2 Government Secrets

1. Capernaum, the main centre of Jesus' ministry in this period, was a relatively important town of perhaps 10,000 inhabitants. But

the Gospels do not record any visit by Jesus to Sepphoris or
Tiberias, the two successive capitals of the Galilean kingdom of
Herod Antipas.

2. The phrase used in 3.21 (*hoi par' autou*) does not necessarily
    mean his family, but may be rendered 'those of his circle', which
    could refer to friends or disciples. It is probable, however, that his
    family are intended because (a) friends and disciples are less likely
    to think him mad, and (b) the arrival of his mother and brothers in
    verse 31 would follow naturally from their setting out to look for
    him in verse 21, without which it is introduced rather baldly.
    (H. Wansbrough has exploited the ambiguity of *hoi par' autou* to
    propose a quite different interpretation – which has not met with
    much favour – to the effect that 'The crowd came together again,
    . . . and when his followers heard it they went out to calm it [the
    crowd] down, for they said it was out of control with enthusiasm';
    'Mark III.21 — Was Jesus Out of His Mind?', *NTS* 18 (1971–72),
    pp. 233–5.)

3. The point is of course made quite explicit in the parallel in
    Matthew 12.28/Luke 11.20.

4. It is generally supposed that Mark contains little of the actual
    teaching of Jesus. This judgement is understandable when Mark
    is compared with the longer Gospels of Matthew and Luke,
    particularly with Matthew's organization of much of Jesus'
    teaching into five major 'discourses'. But if Mark's Gospel is
    studied in its own right, this judgement needs to be modified, in
    that (a) Mark in his editorial comments and in the titles used of
    Jesus lays more emphasis on the role of Jesus as teacher than
    either of the other Synoptic Gospels, and (b) in fact nearly 50% of
    the text of Mark is devoted to presenting the content, not merely
    the fact, of Jesus' teaching – a not inconsiderable proportion! For
    these data see my discussion 'Mark and the Teaching of Jesus', in
    R. T. France and D. Wenham (ed.), *Gospel Perspectives*, vol. 1
    (Sheffield: JSOT Press, 1980), pp. 101–36. The difference is not
    so much that Mark is less interested in what Jesus taught, but that
    he has not generally collected the teaching material together in
    the way Matthew does. Mark 4.1–34 and 13.1–37 are the two
    sections which correspond most closely to Matthew's 'discourses',
    but Matthew 13 and 24–5 are considerably fuller, while focusing
    around the same material.

5. These are the only six Marcan parables ('metaphors and similes
    excluded') listed by J. Jeremias in *The Parables of Jesus* (ET,

London: SCM Press, 1963), p. 247. Other lists are more comprehensive: D. Wenham, *The Parables of Jesus* (London: Hodder & Stoughton, 1989), pp. 249–50, lists fourteen; J. Drury, *The Parables in the Gospels* (London: SPCK, 1985), p. 171, has eighteen; while R. H. Stein, *An Introduction to the Parables of Jesus* (Philadelphia: Westminster Press, 1981), pp. 22–6, lists ten 'parables in which the term "parable" is used as a designation', one further 'story that is clearly a parable', and six 'possible parables'.

6. C. F. D. Moule, 'Mark 4:1–20 yet once more', in E. E. Ellis and M. Wilcox (ed.), *Neotestamentica et Semitica*, Festschrift for M. Black (Edinburgh: T. & T. Clark, 1969), pp. 96–7.

7. J. I. H. McDonald, in B. D. Chilton and J. I. H. McDonald, *Jesus and the Ethics of the Kingdom* (London: SPCK, 1987), pp. 65–6.

8. The same Marcan emphasis is argued on the grounds of the structure of the parable by W. H. Kelber, *The Kingdom in Mark* (Philadelphia: Fortress Press, 1974), p. 40.

9. For a far more exaggerated account of eschatological fruitfulness, see, e.g., Papias, as quoted by Irenaeus, *Adv. Haer.* V, 33.3f., 'A grain of wheat shall bring forth ten thousand ears, and every ear shall have ten thousand grains . . .' Similarly fantastic yields are part of several rabbinic visions of eschatological blessing. By contrast, the thirty- to a hundredfold yield in Mark is not beyond the bounds of possibility, as P. B. Payne demonstrates from a variety of ancient sources in France and Wenham (ed.), *Gospel Perspectives*, vol. 1, pp. 181–6, *contra* Jeremias, *The Parables of Jesus*, 150.

10. Emphasis on the harvest as *the* point of the parable has been largely due to the influence of Jeremias, *The Parables of Jesus*, pp. 77–9, 149–51. A. Jülicher's pioneering work, *Die Gleichnisreden Jesu*, published in 1888, has had enormous influence; for a brief description and critique, see Stein, *An Introduction to the Parables of Jesus*, pp. 53–8.

11. Moule, 'Mark 4:1–20 yet once more', pp. 109–10.

12. It is not so disreputable in scholarly circles today as it once was to defend the synoptic explanation of the parable of the sower as at least appropriate to the parable, if not actually derived from Jesus himself. See, e.g., Moule's article just cited, and the discussion by B. Gerhardsson, 'The Parable of the Sower and its Interpretation', *NTS* 14 (1967–68), pp. 165–93, concluding that the explanation fits the parable 'as hand fits glove' (though on the basis of an

interpretation in terms of the *Shema* which has not been generally adopted!). A detailed rebuttal of Jeremias' arguments for the secondary nature of the explanation is offered by P. B. Payne, 'The Authenticity of the Parable of the Sower and its Interpretation', in France and Wenham (ed.), *Gospel Perspectives*, vol. 1, pp. 163–207.

13. See W. E. Moore, '"Outside" and "Inside": a Markan Motif', *ExpT* 98 (1986–87), pp. 39–43, for a sustained attempt to interpret the whole Gospel in the light of this contrast. More specifically with regard to our passage, it is well drawn out by Kelber, *The Kingdom in Mark*, pp. 25–7.

14. Mark 4.11 (together with the parallels in Matthew and Luke) is the only use of *mysterion* in the Gospels, though Paul makes significant use of it. While it has often been argued that Paul's usage, and indeed much of his theology, derives from his acquaintance with pagan mystery religions (for a recent and extreme example see H. Maccoby, *The Mythmaker* (London: Weidenfeld & Nicolson, 1986), esp. pp. 16–17, 100–3, 195–7), the idea of divine secrets made known only by special revelation is a thoroughly Jewish one, prominent especially in the book of Daniel, and developed in the interpretative tradition of the Qumran commentators: see G. K. Beale, *The Use of Daniel in Jewish Apocalyptic Literature and in the Revelation of St. John* (Lanham MD: University Press of America, 1984), pp. 12–42.

15. Moule, 'Mark 4:1–20 yet once more', pp. 99–100.

16. Much debate about Mark 4.12 has focused on the conjunction *hina* with which it begins. I am not sure that this discussion has been, or is likely to be, very productive. *Hina* is a final conjunction, and the natural understanding of this clause in grammatical terms is as an expression of purpose. This is the function of *hina* in every other occurrence in Mark, except where it is used to introduce an indirect command, request or wish (e.g. 3.9; 5.18, 43; 6.8, 12, 25, etc.; in 5.23 it introduces what is in effect an imperative), and this latter usage in no way reduces its purposive force. Strict syntax is not therefore very promising for the attempt to weaken the 'predestinarian' thrust of Mark 4.12 by rendering *hina* by something other than 'in order that' (though perhaps we might be on more promising ground in observing the two uses of *hina* in 4.22 which do not so much indicate either purpose or result, but rather *necessary sequence*: whatever is hidden 'is bound to' be revealed).

But in any case, if Moule is right about the meaning of Isaiah 6.9–10, we need to look less in the direction of formal syntax and more in that of the overall dynamic of the passage. One proposal worth investigation is that the language both of Isaiah and of Mark should be understood as *ironical*, since irony conveys its message by saying the opposite of what is intended – and thus runs the risk of being seriously misunderstood by those who fail to recognize the mode of communication which is being employed. See, e.g., B. Hollenbach, 'Lest They Should Turn and be Forgiven: Irony', *Bible Translator* 34 (1983), pp. 312–21, who concludes by recommending that translators render Mark 4.12 as follows: '. . . so that they may indeed see but not perceive, and may indeed hear but not understand; because the last thing they want is to turn and have their sins forgiven!'.

17. Moule, 'Mark 4:1–20 yet once more'. The whole article contributes to this argument, which is introduced on pp. 98–9.

18. W. Wrede, *The Messianic Secret* (ET, London: James Clarke, 1971; German original 1901).

19. A selection of responses to Wrede is offered in C. Tuckett (ed.) *The Messianic Secret* (London: SPCK, 1983), among which that by J. Dunn (more fully published as 'The Messianic Secret in Mark', *Tyndale Bulletin* 21 (1970), pp. 92–117) offers a perceptive and wide-ranging critique.

20. Stein, *An Introduction to the Parables of Jesus*, pp. 33–4, gives unusual prominence to this factor as an explanation for the 'concealing' function of Jesus' parables.

3 Revolutionary Government

1. See above p. 22 with reference to D. Wenham, *The Parables of Jesus* (London: Hodder & Stoughton, 1989), especially pp. 20–5.

2. For a stimulating defence of the use of 'revolutionary' to describe the nature of Jesus' message, see H. Gollwitzer, 'Liberation in History', *Interpretation* 28 (1974), esp. pp. 410–12.

3. E. Best, *The Temptation and the Passion: The Marcan Soteriology* (Cambridge University Press, 1963), chapter 1, argued that in the light of 3.27 we should understand Mark as presenting the battle as already won in 1.12–13, so that Satan is now 'bound' and helpless for the period of Jesus' ministry. But it is not clear that 3.27 must refer to a decisive past incident, rather than to a general principle that Satan must be immobilized if his work is to be destroyed. Most scholars see this immobilization as happening

progressively through the conflicts with demonic power which the Gospel records, rather than already completed in the initial encounter. A useful survey of discussion on this point has been provided in an unpublished PhD dissertation by my pupil Estevan Kirschner, *The Place of the Exorcism Motif in Mark's Christology, with special reference to Mark 3:22-30* (CNAA/London Bible College, 1988), pp. 66–72.

4. See Kirschner, ibid., p. 156, for the observation that 'whereas both Matthew and Luke have the *positive* inference that Jesus' exorcisms . . . signal the arrival of the Kingdom of God (Mt. 12.28 and Lk. 11.20) Mark emphasizes the *negative* implication, *viz.* that Satan's *kingdom* (rule, sphere of influence) is being broken down'.

5. *The Upside-down Kingdom* is the title of a study of the kingdom of God in the Synoptic Gospels by D. B. Kraybill (Scottdale PA: Herald Press, 1978), which aims to highlight the uncomfortable practical implications for Christians today of taking seriously Jesus' assault on many accepted values of human society.

6. Gollwitzer, 'Liberation in History', p. 411.

7. So most notably T. J. Weeden, 'The Heresy which Necessitated Mark's Gospel', *ZNW* 59 (1968), pp. 148–58; idem, *Mark: Traditions in Conflict* (Philadelphia: Fortress Press, 1971).

8. E. Best, *Following Jesus* (Sheffield: JSOT Press, 1981), presented as a study of 'Discipleship in the Gospel of Mark', is in fact for the most part a study of 8.27—10.45, regarded as a relatively self-contained section of the Gospel dealing primarily with discipleship. Best assumes (p. 15), rightly as far as I am aware, that this is now the generally accepted interpretation.

9. Best, ibid., 134–45 discusses the various ways in which this interpretation of 8.22–6 and 10.46–52 has been developed.

10. The classic presentation of the rival teaching of Shammai and Hillel on divorce is in Mishnah, *Gittin* 9.10.

11. Josephus' paraphrase of Deuteronomy 24.1–4 is revealing: 'He who desires to be divorced from the wife who is living with him for whatsoever cause – and with mortals many such may arise – must certify in writing . . .' (*Ant.*, IV, 253).

12. 'As a child' may be read as either subjective ('as a child receives it') or objective ('as one receives a child'). The former reading is assumed by most commentators (and is found in a roughly parallel passage in Matt. 18.3), but it is worth remembering that in 9.37 Jesus has spoken of 'receiving a child' as the means of receiving

both himself and the one who sent him. On that reading the child would become an image not only for the subjects of the kingdom of God (v. 14) but also for the kingdom of God itself (v. 15). One of the few commentators to entertain this possibility is H. Anderson, *The Gospel of Mark*, New Century Bible (London: Marshall, Morgan & Scott, 1976), pp. 246–7. See however the comments of J. I. H. McDonald in B. D. Chilton and J. I. H. McDonald, *Jesus and the Ethics of the Kingdom* (London: SPCK, 1987), p. 86.

13. See M. Hengel, *Property and Riches in the Early Church* (ET, London: SCM Press, 1974), pp. 19–22.

14. The romantic speculation that the reference was to a narrow gate at Jerusalem called 'The Needle's Eye' has no foundation in fact (see K. E. Bailey, *Through Peasant Eyes* (Grand Rapids: Wm B. Eerdmans, 1980), p. 166). Other prosaic attempts to evade the force of Jesus' vivid image are even less successful. A comparable rabbinic illustration of an impossibility is of an elephant going through the eye of a needle (Babylonian Talmud, *Berakoth* 55b).

15. See, e.g., the commentaries of V. Taylor, C. E. B. Cranfield, D. E. Nineham, W. L. Lane, C. S. Mann. J. Gnilka, *Das Evangelium nach Markus,* vol. 2 (EKK. Köln: Benziger Verlag, 1979), understands verse 31 as introducing a note of 'surprise', and a warning to the leaders in the Christian community.

16. The extension of the washing rules from priests to lay people was probably quite recent, and still observed mainly if not solely by the Pharisaic schools, not by all lay people. See S. Westerholm, *Jesus and Scribal Authority* (Lund: Gleerup, 1978), pp. 72–4; R. J. Banks, *Jesus and the Law in the Synoptic Tradition* (Cambridge University Press, 1975), pp. 133–4; more fully R. P. Booth, *Jesus and the Laws of Purity* (Sheffield: JSOT Press, 1986), Part II, esp. pp. 189–203.

17. See Mishnah *Tohoroth* 7.6 for the defiling effect of the presence of a tax-collector, and *Demai* 2.2–3 for the requirement that members of Pharisaic *haberoth* must avoid being the guest of an *Am-haaretz*, who is not ritually pure.

18. cf. J. Riches, *Jesus and the Transformation of Judaism* (London: Darton, Longman & Todd, 1980), pp. 104–6.

19. B. F. Meyer, *The Aims of Jesus* (London: SCM Press, 1979), pp. 130–2.

20. E. P. Sanders, 'Jesus and the Sinners', *JSNT* 19 (1983), pp. 5–36; idem, *Jesus and Judaism* (London: SCM Press, 1985), pp. 174–211.

21. See, e.g., M. Hengel, *Victory over Violence* (ET, London: SPCK, 1975), p. 59, and n.74.

22. Josephus, *War*, II, 118, 433; *Antiquities*, XVIII, 4–5, 23–4.

23. So A. Trocmé, *Jesus Christ and the Non-violent Revolution* (ET, Scottdale PA: Herald Press, 1974), followed by J. H. Yoder, *The Politics of Jesus* (Grand Rapids: Wm B. Eerdmans, 1972), esp. pp. 34–40, 64–77.

24. See my study specifically in relation to the issue of wealth, 'God and Mammon: the Practical Relevance of the Teaching of Jesus', *EQ* 51 (1979), pp. 3–21.

4 Government and Power

1. The parallels in Matthew 26.64 and Luke 22.69 both make the time-scale explicit by their inclusion of *ap' arti* and *apo tou nyn* respectively; each phrase means clearly 'from now on', despite the attempt of some English versions to remove the temporal immediacy in Matthew ('hereafter', RSV; 'in the future', Phillips, NIV).

2. For a useful survey of recent discussion of this verse, see K. Brower, 'Mark 9:1 Seeing the Kingdom in Power', *JSNT* 6 (1980), pp. 17–26.

3. B. D. Chilton has made the ingenious suggestion that 'those standing here' refers not to ordinary historical people but to Elijah and Moses, who are about to appear with Jesus in the next scene (9.4), and who are famous in Jewish tradition precisely as those who (with Enoch) did not 'taste death', but were removed from the earthly scene in a more mysterious way; B. D. Chilton, *God in Strength* (Sheffield: JSOT Press, 1987), pp. 267–70; idem, 'An Evangelical and Critical Approach to the Sayings of Jesus', *Themelios* 3 (1978), pp. 83–5. Most critics have found Chilton's proposal more ingenious than convincing, particularly since it is based not on the current form of the text but on his own reconstruction of what he regards as its original form. See further Brower, 'Mark 9:1 Seeing the Kingdom in Power', pp. 30–2.

4. E. Trocmé, *The Formation of the Gospel according to Mark* (ET, London: SPCK, 1975), p. 123, n.1, suggests that Mark's intention in joining 9.1 to 8.34–8 is not to offer assurance in the face of persecution, but rather warning: 'Among those here present there are cowards who would never be willing to die before the end of the world, who avoid taking risks so that they may be alive to see the great Day come!' See further his article 'Marc 9,1: prédiction

ou réprimande?', *Studia Evangelica* II (TU 87. Berlin: Akademie Verlag, 1964), pp. 259–65.

5. Brower, 'Mark 9:1 Seeing the Kingdom in Power', pp. 37–41.

6. Brower, ibid., pp. 21–3 cites me as espousing this interpretation, on the basis of a comment in my *Jesus and the Old Testament* (London: Tyndale, 1971), p. 140, that it was 'tempting'! At that time I was indeed drawn to this suggestion, largely because I wished to read the allusion to Daniel 7.13 in the preceding verse in the light of the further allusion to the same passage in 13.26, where the explicit context is Jesus' prediction of the destruction of the temple. I still believe that Mark 13.26 refers, as its context requires, to the destruction of the temple, but would not now be so strongly 'tempted' to transfer the same reference into this passage, where no such reference is explicit, as will be clear from what follows.

7. The reference is to Exodus 24.16, where this is the period *during which* the cloud of divine glory covered Mount Sinai, at the end of which God spoke to Moses out of the cloud. The parallels are obvious, if not exact, and the whole scene, with a chosen companion accompanying Moses up the mountain while the elders stayed below, followed by glory, cloud and heavenly voice, must have appealed irresistibly to anyone who knew the transfiguration story, especially since Moses is at the centre of them both.

8. E. Best, *Disciples and Discipleship* (Edinburgh: T. & T. Clark, 1986), pp. 214–15; idem, *Following Jesus* (Sheffield: JSOT Press, 1981), p. 55.

9. Thus W. L. Lane, *The Gospel According to Mark* (Grand Rapids: Wm B. Eerdmans, 1974), p. 317, sees the six days as referring back 'to the whole complex of teaching which followed Peter's affirmation of Jesus' messianic dignity, and more particularly to the solemn promise of Ch. 9:1'. Similarly C. E. B. Cranfield, *The Gospel According to Saint Mark* (Cambridge University Press, 1959), pp. 287–9, and other commentators.

10. C. K. Barrett, *Jesus and the Gospel Tradition* (London: SPCK, 1967), p. 85.

11. Among the many suggestive connotations in the appearance of Elijah and Moses with Jesus on the mountain, probably the most immediately obvious to a first-century Jew would have been the fact that these two men, who both disappeared from the earth in mysterious ways (2 Kings 2.11–12; Deut. 34.5–6), were expected to return to inaugurate the great Day of the Lord. This expectation,

based on Malachi 4.5–6 for Elijah and Deuteronomy 18.15ff. for Moses, developed further in post-biblical Judaism; see *TDNT* II, pp. 931–4; IV, pp. 856–64. For a later expression of the hope of the return of Elijah and Moses together, see *Deuteronomy Rabbah* 3.17.

12. See my *Jesus and the Old Testament* (London: Tyndale, 1971), pp. 136–8. In the light of the extensive discussion of the title 'the Son of Man' since that book was written, it is gratifying that I have seen no reason to alter the view of the origin and significance of the title which I set out there. It has been strengthened especially by the robust common sense of the discussion by C. F. D. Moule, *The Origin of Christology* (Cambridge University Press, 1977), pp. 11–22, with his insistence that the definite article ('*the* Son of Man') be taken seriously, and the suggestion that it functions virtually as a demonstrative, pointing to '*that* "son of man"', viz. the human figure presented so memorably in Daniel 7.13.

13. See my *Jesus and the Old Testament*, pp. 210–11 for patristic understanding of Daniel 7, and ibid., pp. 202–4 for the few allusions to Daniel 7 in the New Testament outside the gospel records of Jesus' teaching. For further comments on the shift of usage from Jesus to subsequent Christian use of Daniel 7, see ibid., pp. 215–17, 220–2.

14. W. D. Davies, *The Setting of the Sermon on the Mount* (Cambridge University Press, 1963), p. 197.

15. See especially the study by D. M. Hay, *Glory at the Right Hand: Psalm 110 in Early Christianity* (New York: SBL, 1973).

16. See above, note 1.

17. G. R. Beasley-Murray, *Jesus and the Kingdom of God* (Grand Rapids: Wm B. Eerdmans/Exeter: Paternoster Press, 1986), p. 300. This shift is usually traced to the influence of the work of T. F. Glasson and J. A. T. Robinson. For a brief account of the discussion up to the mid-1960s, see my *Jesus and the Old Testament*, pp. 140–2; for more recent developments, see Beasley-Murray, *Jesus and the Kingdom of God*, pp. 300–4. Beasley-Murray himself, while wishing to retain a reference to the parousia, does not see the sitting and the coming as two separate stages; 'rather they [the versions of Mark and Matthew] declare that the Jewish leaders will experience a revelation of Jesus as the enthroned Son of Man' (p. 303). The recent commentary of C. S. Mann roundly declares, 'Our ears have been so attuned over

the centuries to hear this in terms of a "Second Coming" that we need to be reminded that in Daniel the "coming" is *to* the Lord of Time. It is not coming to earth in some spectacular descent from above' (*Mark*, Anchor Bible (New York: Doubleday, 1986), p. 626).

18. cf. C. S. Mann, ibid., 532 for a similar inference: 'The language of this verse, like 14:62, does not in our view encompass any expectation on the part of Jesus of a return to the scene of his ministry in exaltation-glory.'

19. *Jesus and the Old Testament*, Appendix A (pp. 227–39). The exegesis was, of course, dependent on the study of Jesus' use of Old Testament texts, especially Daniel 7.13–14, in the main argument of the book.

20. For instance, I would no longer wish to maintain that the *angeloi* of verse 27 are human messengers, nor do I think that my understanding of the passage is inappropriate to the normal meaning of 'angels'. For a sympathetic but negative critique of my exegesis of the chapter as a whole, see the article by my colleague David Wenham in H. H. Rowdon (ed.), *Christ the Lord: Studies in Christology presented to Donald Guthrie* (Leicester: IVP, 1982), pp. 138–42. Much of his argument assumes, on the basis of subsequent Christian usage, that the 'natural' understanding of 'coming' language is in reference to the parousia, whereas it is just this assumption which my approach calls in question; such an understanding, I suggest, would not have been at all 'natural' for Jews who knew Daniel 7 and who had not been conditioned by Christian tradition. A less sympathetic critique by M. Casey, *Son of Man* (London: SPCK, 1979), pp. 172–6 roundly asserts that Daniel 7.13 itself describes an earthward 'coming' and that all references to such a coming in the New Testament must be understood as parousia predictions; he makes no allowance for the sort of flexibility in application of Daniel's vision for which I am arguing in this chapter. Both Wenham and Casey in their different ways show how my approach to Mark 13 will not work *given the traditional Christian understanding of language about the coming of the Son of Man*; but it is precisely that traditional understanding that I wish to question, and neither seems to me to have been able to detach themselves from that presupposition.

21. See below, p. 129 (Appendix) for a simple analysis of the indicators of time and sequence in the passage. This analysis has added to my conviction that the direct answer to the disciples' question in

verse 4 is to be found in verses 26–7, not in an earlier part of the discourse.

22. At this point of course the parallel in Matthew is different. For an exegesis of the chapter in Matthew, which takes account of the specifically Matthean features but retains the same overall interpretative framework, see my *The Gospel according to Matthew* Tyndale New Testament Commentaries (Leicester: IVP, 1985), pp. 333–49.

23. Recent discussion of Mark 13 has focused strongly on this aspect of the 'cooling' of apocalyptic fervour, so that the chapter is seen less as an apocalyptic tract and more as a warning against unhealthy apocalypticism. So especially M. D. Hooker, 'Trial and Tribulation in Mark XIII', *BJRL* 65 (1982–83), pp. 78–99.

24. See the full discussion in my *Jesus and the Old Testament*, pp. 233–9.

25. For the background and meaning of *palingenesia*, see *TDNT* I, pp. 686–9.

26. See, e.g., J. Jeremias, *The Eucharistic Words of Jesus* (ET, London: SCM Press, 1966), pp. 217–18. For the significance of 'new', see *TDNT* III, pp. 449–50.

27. See A. M. Ambrozic, *The Hidden Kingdom: A Redaction-Critical Study of the References to the Kingdom of God in Mark's Gospel* (Washington DC: Catholic Biblical Association of America, 1972), pp. 200–1, for the significance of the juxtaposition of verse 24 (the cup of death) with verse 25 (the cup of future glory), as an expression of Mark's continuing theme of the contrast between the present (hidden) and future (glorious) aspects of the kingdom of God.

28. See Cranfield, *The Gospel According to Saint Mark*, p. 428.

5 'The Government Upon His Shoulder'

1. Luke 1.32–3 is the only New Testament passage where an allusion to the wording of Isaiah 9.6–7 seems likely.

2. The significance of the divide between Galilee and Judaea is being increasingly noticed in modern New Testament scholarship. See, e.g., G. Vermes, *Jesus the Jew* (London: Collins, 1973), chapter 2; E. M. Meyers and J. F. Strange, *Archaeology, the Rabbis and Early Christianity* (London: SCM Press, 1981), chapter 2; S. Freyne, *Galilee, Jesus and the Gospels* (Dublin: Gill & Macmillan, 1988).

3. Both Matthew 21.4–5 and John 12.14–16 make the allusion

explicit, but Mark's narrative leaves little room for doubt that this was what Jesus intended. It was hardly necessity which caused him to ride these final two miles after two or three years of itinerant ministry on foot. It was a conspicuous act, since Mishnah *Hagigah* 1.1 suggests that Passover pilgrims were expected to arrive in Jerusalem on foot. And the instructions of Mark 11.2–3, with the agreed 'password', indicate a prearranged plan, designed to make a point.

4. G. Theissen, *The Shadow of the Galilean* (ET, London: SCM Press, 1987).

5. The reading of Matthew 27.16–17 which gives Barabbas' first name as Jesus is rightly adopted by NEB and GNB; the comments by Origen make it clear that this was the standard reading in the early third century, subsequently suppressed for reasons of Christian sensitivity. See further B. M. Metzger, *A Textual Commentary on the Greek New Testament* (London: UBS, 1971), pp. 67–8. For the commonness of the name Jesus in first-century Palestine see above chapter 1, n.2.

6. The importance of Jesus' perceived 'anti-temple' stance as a major factor in his rejection by leaders and people alike has been noted especially by B. F. Meyer, *The Aims of Jesus* (London: SCM Press, 1979), esp. pp. 181–5, 197–202, and by E. P. Sanders, *Jesus and Judaism* (London: SCM Press, 1985), esp. pp. 61–76, 270–1, 287. For the continuing political importance of this issue, see Acts 6.13–14.

7. See especially the detailed study by D. Juel, *Messiah and Temple: the Trial of Jesus in the Gospel of Mark* (Missoula: Scholars Press, 1977).

8. The less direct responses in the parallels in Matthew and Luke mark an element of reluctance to accept the terminology used by the high priest, with its inevitably nationalistic implications, but are none the less clearly affirmative; see D. R. Catchpole, 'The Answer of Jesus to Caiaphas (Matt xxvi.64)', *NTS* 17 (1970–71), pp. 213–26. The same concern is demonstrated by Jesus' immediate shift from 'Messiah' to 'Son of Man' in all three accounts.

9. ibid., 226. The formula is essentially the same as that used in Matthew's version of the Sanhedrin trial, Matthew 26.64.

10. For a sensitive account of the implications of Jesus' temple-cleansing in the context of Jewish nationalism and eschatology, see Meyer, *The Aims of Jesus*, pp. 197–202.

11. Temple, 11.11; fig tree, 11.12–14; temple, 11.15–19; fig tree, 11.20–5; temple, 11.27ff.; contrast Matthew 21.12–22, where the two events stand simply side by side. The symbolic significance of the fig tree episode is agreed by most commentators; see especially the full discussion by W. R. Telford, *The Barren Temple and the Withered Tree* (Sheffield: JSOT Press, 1980).

12. For the fruitless fig tree as a symbol of fruitless Israel in the Old Testament, see Jeremiah 8.13; Micah 7.1; and cf. Jesus' parable of the fruitless fig tree in Luke 13.6–9.

13. There may be a deliberate echo of Ezekiel's vision of the glory of the Lord leaving the temple by the east gate and going to rest on the Mount of Olives, the mark of God's abandonment of his house to destruction (Ezek. 10.18–19; 11.22–3).

14. The temple 'not made with hands' recalls the vision of Daniel 2, where it was a stone 'cut by no human hand' (2.34, 45) which represented the divinely instituted order which was to supplant the existing human power structures.

15. The twelve were called as Jesus' closest companions during his Galilean ministry, and what meagre details we know of them suggest that they were local men. Eight of them are specifically presented as members of the same Galilean family groups or local residents (Mark 1.16–20; 2.13–14; 15.40–1; John 1.44; 2.1–2; 21.2), and while we know nothing specifically of the backgrounds of the others, the twelve as a whole were recognized as a Galilean group (14.70). The name Iscariot, however, while it has been given many interpretations, is widely thought (following several early Greek manuscripts) to represent Ish-Kerioth, 'man of Kerioth'; two towns of that name are known, one in Judaea, the other in southern Transjordan (Moab).

16. L. W. Hurtado, *One God, One Lord: Early Christian Devotion and Ancient Jewish Monotheism* (London: SCM Press, 1988) provides a detailed study of 'chief agents' of God in various strands of Jewish thought, under three headings: 'personified divine attributes', exalted patriarchs and principal angels. Hurtado concludes that the cultic veneration of any of these figures remained impossible in pre-Christian Jewish devotion.

17. ibid., chapter 5. The metaphor of 'mutation' is explained and defended on p. 162, n.20. Hurtado uses the term 'binitarian' extensively to characterize the earliest Christian adaptation of monotheism, but unfortunately it falls outside his brief to trace the further development to a doctrine of the Trinity.

18. I refer here not only to the more commonly cited 'Christological hymns' of Philippians 2.6–11 and Colossians 1.15–20, but also to probable echoes of confessional formulae such as Romans 1.3–4, and to the remarkable 'Marana tha' of 1 Corinthians 16.22, where the use (in a letter to a Greek church) of an Aramaic formula of prayer to Jesus as 'Lord' indicates that such practice was so early established in the Aramaic-speaking church from which Paul derived it that the Aramaic formula had already passed into international usage.

19. M. Hengel, *The Son of God* (ET, London: SCM Press, 1976) moves strongly in this direction:

> The 'apotheosis of the crucified Jesus' must already have taken place in the forties, and one is tempted to say *that more happened in this period of less than two decades than in the whole of the next seven centuries, up to the time when the doctrine of the early church was completed.* (p. 2; his italics)

20. In 1982 I published an article entitled 'The Worship of Jesus: a Neglected Factor in Christological Debate?', in H. H. Rowdon (ed.), *Christ the Lord: Studies in Christology presented to Donald Guthrie* (Leicester: IVP, 1982), pp. 17–36. A similar perspective was suggested by R. J. Bauckham, 'The Worship of Jesus in Apocalyptic Christianity', *NTS* 27 (1980/1), pp. 322–41. Hurtado, *One God, One Lord*, argues throughout that the veneration of Jesus antedates and gives rise to the use of Christological titles and formulations (see pp. 12–14 and much of chapter 5). A forthcoming book by D. R. de Lacey, *The Mediator: On the Christology of Saint Paul*, argues in a similar direction; chapter 1 is entitled 'Faith before Doctrine'.

21. The evidence is clearly set out and discussed, e.g., by A. W. Wainwright, *The Trinity in the New Testament* (London: SPCK, 1962), pp. 53–74; R. E. Brown, *Jesus: God and Man* (London: Chapman, 1968), pp. 6–28. In several of the passages discussed there are textual variants, which suggest that early copyists still found such language difficult. Sometimes too it is disputed whether the translation which involves calling Jesus 'God' is the right one.

22. The dates of several New Testament books are notoriously difficult to fix, particularly in the light of J. A. T. Robinson's bold attempt to reopen all such questions (*Redating the New Testament* (London: SCM Press, 1976); *The Priority of John* (London: SCM Press, 1985), pp. 67–93). One of the most remarkable such texts

is in fact in Romans, which no one would class as a late work! For a full defence of the reading of Romans 9.5 as speaking of 'Christ who is God over all . . .', see B. M. Metzger, in B. Lindars and S. S. Smalley (ed.), *Christ and Spirit in the New Testament: studies in honour of C. F. D. Moule* (Cambridge University Press, 1973), pp. 95–112; if it were not for the doctrinal implications, it is unlikely that anyone would have disputed that that is the natural reading of the Greek syntax.

23.   For a valuable account of the development of the Christological use and implications of 'Lord', see C. F. D. Moule, *The Origin of Christology* (Cambridge University Press, 1977), pp. 35–44.

24.   Exodus 23.20 was about the angel whom God would send in front of *Israel* on the journey to Canaan. This text was conventionally treated together with Malachi 3.1, which uses similar language (see my *Jesus and the Old Testament* (London: Tyndale, 1971), pp. 242–3), but it is the Malachi text which is the controlling influence in Mark's choice of these words here. For the exegesis of Malachi 3.1 in terms of a forerunner of the coming of God, with no intermediate figure, see ibid., pp. 91–2, n.31; an alternative exegesis proposed by P. A. Verhoef, *The Books of Haggai and Malachi* (Grand Rapids: Wm B. Eerdmans, 1987), pp. 287–90, still envisages no third figure as he believes that the second and third clauses both refer to God. The lack of any intermediate figure in Isaiah 40.3 is undisputed.

25.   Most notably, in recent years, J. W. Bowker, 'The Son of Man', *JTS* 28 (1977), pp. 19–48.

26.   See my survey of Jewish interpretation of Daniel 7 up to the third century AD in my *Jesus and the Old Testament*, pp. 174–5, 179–83, 185–8.

27.   S. Kim, *'The "Son of Man"' as the Son of God* (Tübingen: Mohr, 1983); C. C. Caragounis, *The Son of Man: Vision and Interpretation* (Tübingen: Mohr, 1986) – quotation from the summary on pp. 80–1.

28.   The absence of the phrase 'the Son of God' from this verse in some early witnesses to the text (notably the first draft of Codex Sinaiticus, to which the phrase was subsequently added by a corrector) is probably to be explained as a mechanical error at a stage when the titles were conventionally abbreviated in manuscripts, particularly since six genitives, all with the same *-ou* ending, here stand together, so that a copyist's eye might easily miss out the last two words. The phrase is clearly appropriate not

only to the message of the whole Gospel but more especially to the function of the prologue, with the declaration of the same title as its climax in 1.11.

29. The range of use of 'son of God' language is usefully listed by J. D. G. Dunn, *Christology in the Making* (London: SCM Press, 1980), pp. 14–16.

Appendix

v.2 (No time indicator in prediction)

v.4 <u>WHEN</u>?   (and what will be the sign . . .?)

      v.5 <u>Watch out</u> – it is NOT YET (v.7b)

        v.8 all this only THE BEGINNING

      v.9 <u>Watch out</u> – is is NOT YET

        v.10 gospel to all nations FIRST
        v.13 the 'end' still in the future

    v.14 <u>But when</u> . . . i.e., as opposed to the NOT YET of vv. 5–13,
            here the sequence begins (in 'those days', v.19)

      v.21 <u>At that time</u>   this is not yet the end

      v.23 <u>Watch out</u>   still beware of assuming too much

    v.24 <u>But in those days</u> } reference back
        <u>following that distress</u> } to v.19 –

      so a direct, unbroken sequence from the <u>when</u> of v.14

v.26 <u>And then</u> }
               Here at last is the answer to <u>When</u>?, v.4.
v.27 <u>And then</u> }

    v.28f. The fig tree (a parable of necessary chronological sequence)
        shows that <u>these things</u> indicate that 'it is near'

    v.30f. and therefore <u>all these things</u> must inevitably occur within
        '<u>this generation</u>'.

- -

v.32 '<u>BUT</u> about <u>THAT</u> day or hour . . .'
      WHICH 'day or hour'? – no (singular) day or hour so far mentioned

    v.33 <u>Watch out</u> – it may be ANY time

    vv.32–7 speak throughout of an UNKNOWN time, which comes
        without announcement, in stark contrast to the

           NOT YET
           BUT WHEN } of vv. 5–31.
           THEN
           WITHIN GENERATION

*(Based on the Greek text – some of the phrases quoted are obscured in some
English translations)*

Index of Scripture References

References in bold type are to main discussions of the passage cited

129

Index of Names and Subjects